Container Gardening

Expert advice on creating perfect pots for every situation

Published by
The Reader's Digest Association Limited
London • New York • Sydney • Montreal

Contents

Choosing a style

10 Shapes and effects

12 Materials and textures

14 Window boxes

16 Hanging baskets

18 Learning to use colour

20 Using colour creatively

22 Informal container style

24 Pots at the front door

26 Pots on the patio

28 A water feature in a pot

30 Growing herbs in a pot

32 Growing fruit in a pot

34 Vegetables in a pot

36 Salads in containers

Creating the perfect environment

40 Acid-loving plants

42 Lime-loving plants

44 Plants from the bogs

46 Drought-loving plants

48 Alpines in containers

50 Shade-loving plants

Container Gardening

Containers for every season

54 Spring bulbs

56 Polyanthus

58 Tulips

60 Petunias

62 Summer scent

64 Geraniums

66 Ringing the changes

68 Busy lizzies

70 Autumn warmth

72 Ornamental harvest

74 Winter pansies

76 Christmas pots

78 Winter to spring

Pot practicalities

82 Choosing pots and plants

84 Drainage and compost

86 Mulches

88 Planting mixed containers

90 Planting a hanging basket

92 Watering

94 Maintenance

96 Keep pests at bay

98 Avoiding diseases

100 Container plant directory

125 Index

128 Acknowledgments

Introduction

Do you yearn for the hot baked colours of Provence or the brilliant whitewashed walls and scarlet geraniums that typified that village you loved on a Mediterranean holiday? Do you long for sweetly scented cottage-garden blooms, or the stillness and simplicity of an oriental garden? Whatever your preference, and no matter how small your space or budget, you can create exactly the mood you want with a container garden.

Your particular style may come from a single inspiration such as a powerful childhood memory – the sight of a field of scarlet poppies, say, or the distinctive spicy scent of wallflowers. Perhaps you can still visualise that painted narrowboat with its colour-washed barrels brimming with flowers. With a little careful planning you can create a container garden that not only fulfils your vision, but also thrives in your particular garden environment and local climate. In this book, we show you how to achieve just the effect you want, whether you have a sunny terrace or a windswept balcony, an exposed flat roof or a tiny, shady basement yard.

Choosing a style

Shapes and effects

Looks matter when you choose a pot, but you also have to consider where it will go and what you want to plant in it. A front door might call for a hanging basket to provide colour and fragrance at eye level, while a patio offers space for a variety of containers. Here are shapes for every purpose.

When your starting point is a plant, rather than a location, choose the pot to fit: a hydrangea needs a much larger pot than a geranium. If outdoor space is limited, you may want to plant up one large container, but with more space you can combine pots of varying size and shape to achieve the same effect as a border.

A look to suit the plant

A large pot, because it holds more compost, is ideal for growing an interesting combination of plants. But once planted up, it will be difficult to move. To lighten the load, fill the base of large pots with bits of broken polystyrene plant trays or polystyrene beads. Another advantage of using a large container is that the compost is less likely to freeze around the roots in winter and won't dry out so fast in summer.

Height and stability

Bear in mind the height of the mature planting when choosing a pot. A dwarf or low-growing plant can look swamped in a heavy container, while a large shrub will look badly proportioned in a narrow pot.

Stability is crucial with a tall plant, which may sway in the wind and topple the pot. Containers with very tapered bases are particularly vulnerable. The most stable shapes are square pots, taller containers with wide shoulders, or large, round dishes.

To anchor a pot, drive a stake into the ground, or the space between two paving slabs, place the drainage hole of the pot over the stake then slide the empty pot over it.

Creating a successful display

Consider the form and size of the plants you are choosing, the location and the size and

shape of the pot. Tall pots suit trailing plants such as ivy, creeping Jenny and ground ivy. They are also ideal for lilies or clematis, which both need a deep, cool root run. Shallow containers such as old sinks and alpine dishes are more suited to the delicate shapes of rockery plants, spring bulbs such as crocus, and low-growing herbs.

Tall, elegant, narrow-necked pots make a curvaceous focus on a patio or among other plants. They can look spectacular filled with trailing stems, wispy grasses, or weeping plants. But the narrow necks make it almost impossible to remove a plant for repotting. Big-bellied pots present the same problem, but both can be used as *cachepots*, to disguise a plain plastic pot placed inside the container. Square containers such as wooden Versailles boxes are also often used as *cachepots*. They set off topiary shrubs and trees pruned into formal shapes.

Shallow containers (above, bottom) or hanging baskets make neat homes for alpines and bulbs.

Big-bellied pots (left) in terracotta and bright glazes give plenty of space for large shrubs, such as azalea or rhododendron.

Hard-edged, angular planters (above, top) in metal and wood lend a sense of form and order to a balcony or terrace.

Tall, slender containers (right) such as chimney pots and amphorae show off trailing plants beautifully.

Great plants deserve fine containers and there are many beautiful options. Each material has good points and bad, so discover how to find the best partner for your precious blooms.

Choosing a pot no longer means deciding whether or not you can afford terracotta rather than plastic. Containers are now available in a bewildering array of materials – from galvanised metal containers to bamboo, from glass fibre to glazed ceramic – and there are many ways to achieve a stone effect or bronze finish that doesn't cost a fortune or weigh as much as the real thing.

Because there is so much choice, you need to think about the advantages and disadvantages of the material when you are picking a container. Plastic is light, inexpensive and can be treated to all manner of disguises. Wood, terracotta and stone are good root insulators – against heat or cold – and therefore ideal for plantings in full sun or exposed northerly settings.

Concrete and reconstituted stone pots are strong, frost-resistant and retain heat. Reconstituted stone doesn't weather quickly, so let plants spill over the rim to soften the look. Both come in a wide range of shapes from classical to modern. Glass-fibre pots are also now made to emulate these materials (see pot right).

Terracotta and plastic are the most common materials for pots. Terracotta mellows with age, but is easily chipped or broken. It is porous and drains well, so is ideal for drought-tolerant geraniums or Mediterranean herbs; other plants will need frequent watering. When moistened, terracotta keeps plant roots cool in hot weather. Check that the pot is frost-resistant. If not, you will have to wrap it up, or store the pot indoors for winter. Plastic pots are light and portable and not damaged by frost. As plastic is not porous, compost dries out less quickly. You won't have to water so often but will have to watch out for waterlogging.

Wood and wicker have a lightweight appearance, but many wooden tubs are substantial enough to hold large shrubs. Wood is resistant to frost and insulates plants from extreme heat and cold. Prevent rot by treating the container with a preservative that does not harm plants, or line it with plastic. Stand wooden tubs on bricks to aid drainage: if water collects in them, the wood will rot.

Galvanised metal containers look great in modern settings, such as on decking or gravel beds. But metal is a poor insulator so compost and roots may be baked in hot weather or frozen in winter. You can also get a similar effect with glass-fibre pots made to emulate metal finishes – both modern and classical.

Ceramic or glazed pots are available in a range of colours and patterns. The smooth surface is easy to wipe clean, keeping disease at bay. Ceramic pots need to be moved and filled carefully because they are easily chipped or cracked. Glazed pots are not porous so plants need careful watering to avoid waterlogging. When buying check whether the pot is frost-proof, and that it has drainage holes in the base.

14 Window boxes

Vibrant boxes, alive with colour, will transform a simple windowsill into an eye-catching display of flowers and foliage – from inside and out. Sitting on a sill or fixed to the wall beneath a window, they offer the chance to change the outlook with every season and to enhance the façade of your home.

The most attractive window boxes are often those in which the bright colours and vigour of the plants create a swirling mass that obscures the box and almost envelops the window it is dressing. But if you are attaching a box below a window that opens outwards, be careful to site it low enough, so that you can still open the window when the plants mature.

Window boxes are long, thin, usually not very deep, and hold a relatively small amount of compost, so they need slow-release fertiliser granules, as well as water-retaining gel or granules incorporated into the mix.

Siting and fixing a window box

Make sure that a window box sited on the front of the house is securely fixed with brackets or iron restraints. This will keep it safe from theft and will prevent endangering people walking beneath it.

If you live above other people, or if your window box overhangs a pavement, it may be a good idea to equip the box with a drip tray: it will be no fun for neighbours to be caught under a shower each time you water the plants.

Attach before planting

Try to fix your window box into position before you plant it up – it may be impossibly heavy to move later. If the box is for a ground-floor window it will be easy to work on it from the outside. But if you live higher up, you may need to throw the windows wide open and work from inside.

Too pretty to hide, (top) this picket-fence window box has country cottage charm. Creamy white Asarina procumbens trail through the slats in contrast with the dark red *Lobelia* 'Fan Scharlach' and chocolate cosmos.

A regiment of primulas (middle) lined up along a sill will brighten many a dull winter's day and makes a pretty alternative to a traditional trough.

Strong plants (bottom right) are needed to withstand autumn weather. Here dwarf conifers draw the eye to the glossy pink berries of *Pernettya mucronata* while glowing purple heather makes an appealing miniature hedge.

Plain colour schemes (bottom left) often work best in a confined space like a window box. Here, white begonias and geraniums, with a touch of lilac lobelia, make an elegant summer display.

Creating style on the window sill

Even in the confined space of a window box it is possible to create a variety of styles. A limited palette – one colour plus foliage plants – for example, a rich red geranium with ivy – would provide a vibrant, yet formal style and will have most impact when viewed from a distance. Generously proportioned pastel-toned petunias, with trails of lobelia in complementary colours, and drooping, brilliant-hued fuchsia, suggest a more relaxed, country style.

Silver and grey is a deservedly popular colour combination for foliage in window boxes. Add a white or cream variegated ivy or white-flowered lobelia to add highlights to a cool contemporary display.

For a north-facing window use plants such as ivy, box or vividly coloured busy lizzies (*Impatiens*), which all thrive in shade, as well as ferns – with their geometric shapes – and cyclamen. In boxes which get full sun try the floriferous diascias in a range of pastel colours.

A formal stone trough with its winter display of clipped box can be livened up instantly in spring by tucking a few bright polyanthus in at the front.

Hanging baskets

Suspended anywhere from a door to a tree, baskets of flowers have an old-fashioned appeal. But with the right plants and container, the hanging basket can have a place in even the most modern of settings. Just one carefully considered basket can be enough to add interest to a front entrance.

A successful basket can be so luxuriant in summer that the chains and container are hidden and the whole confection seems to be floating on air. Hanging baskets are the most popular garden ornaments and several matching ones grouped along the front of a house or on a pergola have great dramatic impact. If you are hanging a basket by a door, position it away from head-height.

Plants for a hanging basket

To make watering less arduous, choose plants that will thrive even if water is in short supply. There are numerous drought-tolerant bedding plants, which will flower all summer. Begonias, brachyscome, busy lizzies, felicia, geraniums, nasturtiums, petunias and verbena are all suitable.

A basket does not hold much compost and dries out rapidly, so it should be watered at least once a day. If the basket is out of reach, you will need a long-handled watering device, a bracket that enables you to lower the basket, or a permanent irrigation system.

Holding on to water

There are also a number of ways to increase the water-holding capacity of the compost. Use the largest basket possible: the more compost, the longer it will take to dry out. Use a moisture-retentive liner such as wool, fibre or foam. Cardboard liners are also suitable, and their looks can be improved by covering them with moss. Finally, mix water-retaining gel or granules into the compost.

Trailing campanulas (left) tumbling out of a moss-lined wire basket harmonise with the drooping green leaves of a neighbouring weeping willow.

The classic mixture of white and silver (above) gives this basket its cool simplicity. An underplanting of silvery grey helichrysum frames a froth of *Petunia* 'Ice White'.

Great plants to fill or soften the edges of a hanging basket

Upright plants
- Begonia
- Geraniums
- Heuchera
- Impatiens
- Petunia

Trailing plants
- *Begonia* x *tuberhybrida* 'Pendula'
- *Bidens ferulifolia*
- Campanula
- Fuchsia
- Ivy-leaved geraniums
- *Glechoma hederacea*
- *Helichrysum petiolare* (green and yellow)
- Small leaf or variegated ivies
- Lobelia
- Nasturtium
- Scaevola
- Black-eyed Susan (*Thunbergia alata*)
- Verbena
- Viola

Naturally trailing plants can also be encouraged to climb. Wind their stems around the chains of the basket to give your display added height.

A glowing autumn sumach (right) makes the perfect place to hang a basket of burgundy-leaved *Heuchera* 'Chocolate Ruffles' and orange violas. Change the planting with the seasons to coordinate with the colours of nature.

18 Learning to use colour

Understanding the impact colour can have is a skill. Some people have a natural eye for colour, and mix and match colour schemes by instinct, but most of us have to learn by experimenting to achieve the desired effect. Follow these simple rules for using colour with flair.

A good place to start when choosing schemes for the garden is to use the colour wheel (below), which is based on the natural spectrum of the rainbow.

Schemes in which the use of colour is restrained are usually more successful than those that combine a riot of different colours and shades. The most memorable plantings often use colours that are next to, or close by, each other on the colour wheel. Such neighbouring colours are sympathetic to one another, rather than fighting for attention, and create naturally harmonious planted arrangements.

A harmonious late-summer arrangement could be achieved by filling a dark burgundy container with carmine red and dark cerise dahlias and placing it in front of a

For a successful colour combination (far left) use the wheel as your guide and mix only opposite (complementary) or adjacent (harmonious) shades together. Green is the neutral of the plant world, but can still have impact when used as a contrast to a lighter colour

Team green with neighbouring yellow (left) for a harmonious container display. The old zinc bucket adds a casual touch.

background of maroon-tinged foliage, such as cotinus. Here all the colours are in sympathy because they are close together on the colour wheel. Another way to achieve harmony is to use shades of a single colour.

Creating visual drama

For a dramatic look, choose colours that are directly opposite each other on the colour wheel. These contrasting pairs are known as complementary colours, because they work together to create maximum impact. You could mix yellow and purple using daffodils and irises, or orange and blue by putting nasturtiums with lavender.

Adding a splash of colour

Including a small amount of a contrasting colour in an otherwise harmonious arrangement produces a dash of excitement. The burgundy arrangement described earlier, for instance, would really come alive if you added one or two bright marigolds or orange-centred gazanias to the planting mix.

To achieve the strongest display of pure or saturated colour, pack the container with flowers of similar colours but different shapes. But remember that saturated colour can be tiring after a while, so an arrangement or collection of pots is often more successful if it is broken up with a paler shade, or muted with a darker one.

Calm and collected planting

To create a really restful effect with your container arrangements, combine different flowers in a range of similar colours and tones and use lots of green foliage to give the arrangement natural balance.

The power of white

White is a powerful and eye-catching colour – adding a white flower will give extra definition to almost any display. But it can be overpowering if used in a block, except when adding light to a dark corner. Most white daisies have dark or yellow centres which give relief, but you can also soften the stark effect of an all-white arrangement by including green or silvery foliage, or the velvety, richly coloured leaves of a variegated coleus.

The versatility of container gardening means you can introduce any colour to create the look you desire. One yellow flower can vary widely in shape from another, and each will strike the eye differently, depending on the season. Look beyond the basic colour to see the many effects you can achieve.

Decide what mood you want to create before choosing any plants and pots. Bright yellows, oranges and reds are dominant 'advancing' colours. Blues, mauves and greens are 'receding' colours, because they appear to withdraw into the background. The intensity of natural light should also be considered. Hot and fiery colours have impact in the sun, while at twilight misty blues and mauves radiate a more subtle glow. White flowers and silver foliage are luminous in shade, drawing the eye. White is the perfect colour for plantings that will be seen mainly in the evening.

Creating mood with colour

As a general rule, receding colours can be used together in greater quantity than advancing ones. Shades of pink, tempered with touches of cerise and magenta, would be stimulating but never overpowering. Similarly, a splash of an advancing colour, such as yellow, adds a cheerful and welcoming note to any display, outside a front door, for instance, or for a window box in the depths of winter.

Colour and season

Light alters throughout the year. In spring the soft cool quality of the light suits bright colours – yellow daffodils and red tulips look bright and fresh early in the year where they might look harsh in summer. The pinks, lilacs and mauves so popular in summer containers seem to suit the soft, often hazy light of a sunny British day. And in the darker autumn months, glowing reds and bronzes are particularly effective.

Plant a bouquet in a bucket, (left) mixing shapes and colour. Here, spires of purple lavender, red dianthus and sunny, daisy-like gerberas combine with tumbling nasturtiums for a luxuriant, expansive effect.

The reds and bronzes of heathers add a welcome glow in the fading light of autumn.

Hot colours vibrate in the midday sun and these spring poppies (right) leap from a surrounding sea of silver.

Informal container style

Create the impression of nature running wild for a relaxed, informal look. Choose containers with worn finishes and plants with soft outlines. Whether you live in the town or country, you can create an exuberant and relaxed style of container gardening that gives an atmosphere of unrestrained nature.

The effect to aim for here is a container that looks as if it has been planted haphazardly. The overall shape is crucial: informal designs need to look generous and expansive rather than neat and tidy. And it is usually better if colours harmonise. Informal displays are a great way to emphasise the texture of an arrangement – for instance, by using daisy shapes and bells, spires and soft trailing plants all in the one pot.

Planting an informal display

The best time to assemble such a display is when the plants are small and can be packed tightly into the pot. If you wait until they are large enough to see the flower buds, they will have bigger rootballs and the container will accommodate fewer of them.

The most successful containers for informal arrangements have a neutral finish allowing the plants to shine whatever their colour, shape or size. Informal plantings can lead to the pots being almost invisible, because they are either clustered in a random group or hidden by tumbling greenery.

Casual terracotta

Curvaceous terracotta pots have a romantic, relaxed appearance and their surface improves with the patina of time, which mellows and softens the colour. However, the harsh red of new machine-made pots may be softened instantly with a coat of pale stone paint or limewash. Terracotta is a great medium for experimenting with paint techniques such as colour-washing, dragging or stippling. These give a broken finish, and provide colours and tones that harmonise or contrast with flowers and foliage. Or you could try using stencils to add a border of leaves or flower motif to plain flowerpots.

Other relaxed containers

Wood can also be used effectively in an informal garden – half-barrels may be stained in natural shades or their slats painted to echo the colour scheme of the plants. Both wooden crates and old fruit boxes make attractive homes for herb or vegetable gardens.

Salvaged sinks, stone troughs and galvanised tubs all make terrific wide, low-level planters for a profusion of trailing plants and are great for scattering seeds of colourful annuals that will give a delightfully free effect.

Battered wire baskets
(above) took especially charming
in an informal setting and are
the prettiest way to display
cascading varieties.

Simple stencils (left) have been
used to decorate these three
terracotta pots, brimming with
tufted *Lampranthus spectablis*.

Pots at the front door

It is all too easy to devote your energies to the back garden and ignore the front of the house. But, whether your ideal is roses round the door or a more formal effect, it is good to give your front door a welcoming look. Pots come into their own, giving a flexible display that you can change with the seasons.

Your choice of containers and plants will be determined, in part, by the architecture of your home and the style of the front door – although, if you live by a busy road, you may be wise to consider pollution-tolerant species, such as cranesbills, geum and *Veronica*.

A formal style

The formal doorways of many town houses call for a symmetrical design, and a pair of plants in matching planters is often the best option here. Choose conifers or lollipop bays for all-year effect, fuchsias or standard marguerites for a lighter summer touch. Square terracotta pots or Versailles planters work particularly well in a setting like this.

Working with colour

Alternatively, you might be guided by colour, choosing a scheme that tones with the door itself, opting for all white, or using foliage with different textures, shapes and hues.

If you don't have a porch, you can create pillars using flowers instead. Place half-barrels filled with summer bedding plants on either side of the door and suspend hanging baskets above them. Then train annual climbers such as canary creeper to grow up strips of trellis fixed to the walls behind the barrels.

Keeping containers safe and secure

Containers are particularly vulnerable to theft, so you may wish to consider using less expensive glass fibre or plastic pots in an exposed front garden. Alternatively, you can secure planters with chains and rings set into the wall, or deter thieves by driving a stake through a drainage hole in the base of the pot.

Warm autumn colour (top left) welcomes the visitor to this front door. A bronze-leafed berberis and a stunning weeping cotoneaster, laden with a berry feast, are underplanted with brilliant red cyclamen.

Matching pairs of sculptural plants (bottom left) in urns dressed the entrance to many a stately home. Here, a pair of standard fuchsias in steel boxes provide a modern interpretation of a traditional decorative style.

Aromatic plants (right) give visitors an old-fashioned scented welcome and perfume the house when you open the door. Fill summer pots with regal lilies, try scented hyacinth and narcissi for spring, or encourage fragrant honeysuckle, jasmine or roses in pots to scramble around the door.

Pinks and blues (below) are used to charming and unpretentious effect. A blue galvanised pot echoes the glossy door, while a creamy band painted round the top of a terracotta pot picks up the colours of the tiles and grout.

26 Pots on the patio

Summertime is the season when a terrace comes into its own. A patio may be part of a bigger garden, or a paved courtyard may be all you have. Whatever its surroundings, an area of brick or stone paving, gravel or decking can become a welcoming haven with carefully chosen containers.

As a general rule, the most successful groupings combine one or two large pots with various smaller containers. Too many little pots distract the eye and make for a disjointed effect.

A big shrub or tree creates a focus and is a good starting point for a terrace design. They also look good viewed from inside on a winter's day, whether covered in pretty evergreen foliage or with their bare branches outlined in frost.

Scented patio pots

A sunny terrace is a great place for scented plants – the warmth will enhance their scent and the blooms will attract lazy humming bees and bright butterflies. Herbs do especially well in sunny corners – thyme, marjoram, rosemary and sage have aromatic leaves that will scent the air if you brush against them.

Try adding a trellis to a tub and grow summer jasmine (*Jasminum officinale*) up it. The mock orange blossom (*Philadelphus* 'Beauclerk') emits a heady citrus scent in the early evening while an even richer fragrance is given off at twilight by the white trumpets of the tobacco plant (*Nicotiana alata*).

Colour on a patio

You can achieve a stylish look by choosing just one or two colours for your plantings, or using similar pots. But don't be too strict – a cool theme of blues, lilacs and mauves, a warm theme of reds, yellows and oranges, or a mix of the palest pastels and whites will all give a sense of unity.

Bring sunlight to a shady patio with greeny yellows, whites and glossy foliage planted in warm-toned terracotta pots. Cool corners can be enlivened with sculptural ferns and variegated ivies, and the cheerful colours of busy lizzies, which thrive happily in shade.

A patio kitchen garden

One of the prettiest as well as most rewarding patio plants is the tomato, and it is easy to raise in a grow bag. To prevent your colour scheme being spoilt by the bag's garish print, hide it in a log-roll box. Strawberry planters are always pretty, and you could grow a tangle of runner beans and sweet peas up a wigwam of canes in a sunny corner. If you have enough space, a dwarf fruit tree in a pot will add structure as well as giving you an autumn treat.

Move your pots around

One of the best things about containers is that they are not static. If one plant looks miserable, you change it for another healthier specimen; as an arrangement passes its best, you can hide it behind another that is starting to bloom. Move the pots about to suit your mood, the occasion, the best interests of the plants and to maintain year-round visual interest.

Out of the glasshouse

A sheltered patio also makes a good summer home for container-grown conservatory specimens and house plants. Varieties such as *Abutilons*, agapanthus, citrus trees, cordylines, tender fuchsias and geraniums, olive trees, most palms and tree ferns are fine outside in summer and will provide an exotic contrast to the hardier plants that surround them outdoors.

In a city garden (left) the owner has made the best use of the walls by hanging pots of brilliant red geraniums. On the ground are tubs of lobelia and petunias in softly coordinating colours.

A glorious blue urn (far left) gives weight to an informal arrangement of fragile angelonias, penstemons and 'Million Bells' petunias. The colour is carried through to the chair beyond.

A water feature in a pot

For an instantly tranquil effect, nothing beats a water feature. Even the smallest garden has space for a pond or other water feature in a pot. Make a lily pond in a half-barrel or stand a tinkling fountain, splashing the leaves of waterside plants, on your patio and enjoy the calm.

Moving water adds interest in a garden and makes a welcome change of appearance in a bank of greenery. The first thing you will need is a watertight container. Most stone and glazed terracotta pots have drainage holes already drilled in them, but aquatic centres and large garden centres may stock them intact. Plastic containers may be an easier option, since they tend to be sold with holes marked, but not punched out. Old wooden beer barrels make excellent ponds when they have been waterproofed on the inside with a sheet of tough pond liner.

Water-loving plants

It is possible to make a very attractive, contemporary-looking water feature for your garden without including plants. But, there are many beautiful species that will thrive in watery conditions.

Plants such as the *Houttuynia cordata* 'Chameleon' and *Oenanthe javanica* 'Flamingo' in the fountain bowl (top right) are happy with their roots in water and with their foliage being splashed. *Lysimachia* and *Mimulus* will also stand up to being splashed – *Mimulus* are often found by streams – but thrive best if not actually standing in water.

Plants to add oxygen

Any successful pond needs at least one oxygenating plant, such as hair grass (*Eleocharis acicularis*), hornwort (*Ceratophyllum demersum*), milfoil (*Myriophyllum spicatum*) or water crowfoot (*Ranunculus aquatilis*) and a surface-floating plant to cast shade such as as frogbit (*Hydrocharis morsus*), pygmy water lilies (*Nymphaea* 'Pygmaea Rubra'; *N.* 'Pygmaea alba') and water soldiers (*Stratiotes aloides*).

A half-barrel makes a perfect pond, (far left) deep enough to grow water lilies and wide enough to accommodate a good balance of different plants. You could even include a couple of goldfish in a tub this size for their flashes of gold.

A spreading dwarf water lily and tall cyperus (left) are happy here in their blue glazed pond. Raising a container pond off the ground on pot feet or upturned flowerpots will help to keep it from freezing in winter.

A spray of water catches the light and adds a sparkle to this display (above). Choose water-tolerant species, such as *Houttuynia* and *Oenanthe* (variegated water dropwort) for the fountain container.

30 Growing herbs in a pot

If you like to cook with herbs but do not have much space in the garden, you can still grow them using pots and window boxes. Their beautiful foliage makes a pleasing alternative to summer flowers and their scented leaves have a sensory impact whenever you open the window or go out on the patio.

The best herbs for containers are those you use regularly but in small amounts; when you want large handfuls of parsley for a fish sauce or basil to make pesto, it is better to buy a bunch than to strip the leaves from an entire plant.

Containers for growing herbs

As a rule, herbs look best in traditional pots. Ceramic, terracotta, stone, lead or wood will all add to the tranquil feeling that herbs give to an area. Make sure the container has lots of drainage holes before you start to plant it and position it near a sunny seat if you want to enjoy the fragrance.

To grow a collection of culinary herbs in a very small space, a strawberry or herb pot is a good choice. Depending on size, it will hold four to eight herbs around the sides and up to three in the top. When you are planting several herbs in a single pot, choose varieties that do not grow too quickly and avoid mint, which can overwhelm a mixed container in a matter of weeks. All mints are better confined to individual pots.

Consider the look of the plant

Before you pot, consider the shape of the plant and the colour and texture of its leaves. Most culinary herbs have variegated forms, or varieties with leaves in gold, silver-grey, blue, purple or cream as well as green. It is easy to find herbs that look beautiful and still retain all their flavour.

Basil (above) thrives in small pots on a kitchen windowsill or in the kitchen itself. Cut as needed for the freshest leaves.

A window box decorated with lead flashing (right) looks soft and pretty and brings its cargo of herbs within cutting distance.

Potted herbs (far right) are surrounded by a sea of free-growing alliums (wild garlic) in a country cottage herb garden.

Tall herbs, such as angelica, fennel and lovage, make an impressive display planted one or two to a pot and placed where they can make a bold statement. They need a pot big and heavy enough to balance their height and remain stable in windy weather.

Some shrubby herbs, such as rosemary and bay, make sizeable plants and can be trained into pyramids, balls or informal half-standards. Once established, they will not need to be repotted for several years.

Growing tips

Herbs grow best in well-drained soil, so add one part sharp sand to four parts compost, or a core of grit. Plant in late spring or early summer and give a balanced liquid plant food weekly from six weeks after planting. Annual and biennial herbs such as basil, dill and parsley, need to be replaced every year, but even perennials, such as mint and sage, taste better when they are young, so renew them after three or four years.

Great herbs for containers

- **Basil** cinnamon; liquorice; lemon: lettuce leaved; Minette; Red Rubin; Thai; sweet basil
- **Chives** traditional; garlic
- **Parsley** Curlina; plain leaved; moss curled
- **Lemon balm** common; variegated (*Melissa officinalis* 'Variegata'); golden (*M. officinalis* 'Aurea')
- **Oregano** (pot marjoram) golden (*Origanum onites* 'Aureum'); variegated (*O. onites* 'Variegatum'); compact (*O. onites* 'Compactum')
- **Sage** common; purple (*Salvia officinalis* 'Purpurascens'); golden (*S. officinalis* 'Icterina'); tricoloured (*S. officinalis* 'Tricolor')
- **Thyme** bushy form: garden thyme dwarf and creeping forms: gold variegated (*Thymus* 'Doone Valley'); lemon-scented golden (*T.* 'Bertram Anderson'); woolly grey thyme (*T. pseudolanuginosus*) wild thyme: (*T. serpyllum*)

Growing fruit in a pot

Fruit grows very well in containers, so if you yearn for the taste of a just-picked strawberry or blackcurrant, here is how to grow your own. Choose the right varieties and keep well-fed and well-watered and you should be rewarded with fresh berries for several months of the year.

Strawberries can be grown in all manner of containers. To enjoy fresh berries over the longest period, either grow perpetual fruiting varieties, which allow you to pick small quantities of fruit all summer long, or plant early, mid season and late varieties separately. This method allows you to harvest more fruit at any one time, but takes up more space.

Starting out with strawberries

The best way to start is to buy pot-grown strawberry plants in spring: five plants are plenty for a hanging basket and ten for the average 35cm pot. Plant them immediately in soil-based compost and they will produce a modest crop in their first year. The second season should see a bumper crop, followed by a slightly lower yield the third summer. Then start again with fresh stock.

Careful watering and feeding are essential. If you are to reap a good crop, you must never let the compost dry out, particularly when the fruit is forming and ripening; if you do, the bulk of your crop will drop off the bush almost immediately. Water well then leave the pots for up to three weeks, until they reach the point of drying out. Be careful not to overwater them during the winter months.

Blueberry bushes and redcurrant bushes will also thrive for many years in large containers. And rhubarb is another great, if unexpected, pot plant, with its wonderful architectural foliage. If you have room in the pot around the fruit bush, you could add almost any decorative bedding plant: the effect will be spectacular.

Growing tips for soft fruit

Most soft fruit thrives best in a soil-based compost: John Innes No.2 for strawberries, and John Innes No.3 for red, white and blackcurrants and for gooseberries. A rhubarb crown needs a good-sized tub or a 60cm pot. The stems can be pulled until early July; then it should be allowed to grow unchecked to build up reserves.

Pruning fruit bushes

Gooseberries and red and white currants should have the side shoots from the main branches shortened and the leader tipped in early autumn. With blackcurrants, take out about a third of the branches at the base of the bush each year to encourage new wood to develop. Pruning the bushes may be done as soon as the crop has been gathered, or left until later in the season.

All soft-fruit bushes need to be watered copiously and fed regularly with a liquid tomato fertiliser, starting when the fruit begins to form and continuing until it is gathered. Blackcurrants are especially attractive to birds and the bushes will need some form of protection.

Pot-grown strawberries (left) won't yield as much fruit as those grown in the ground. The pleasure lies in producing them on your own doorstep.

Rhubarb (above) grows well in most conditions. All it needs is a cool, even damp, place in the sun or semishade. It doesn't need protection against frost in winter, even in the coldest regions as it is a Siberian native.

Blueberries (right) are unusual pot plants. These delicious fruits need a lime-free, humus-rich compost and are more successful if replanted every two to three years.

Vegetables in a pot

Nothing compares with the taste of freshly picked vegetables – and you do not need a lot of expertise to grow them. Beans and peas, tomatoes and salad vegetables are quite easy to raise in pots. Place them close to the kitchen door for easy access to a fresh crop.

Tomatoes are one of the most adaptable container plants. You can grow dwarf or bush varieties in window boxes, hanging baskets or around the edges of pots. Bush tomatoes are best in grow bags or pots at least 30cm across.

Tomatoes and cucumbers

Tomatoes grown on a single stem as cordons need tying to a stake as they grow. Or set pots near a wall or fence and tie the plants to a fixed trellis. This is probably the best way of training the stems of a cucumber, but some outdoor varieties, such as ridge cucumbers, can trail over the side of the pot.

Both tomatoes and cucumbers will thrive only in warm weather and are nearly always killed by frost. If raising from seed, sow straight into the pots outdoors when the temperature rises in spring and there is no risk of frost. But you may find it easier to raise seedlings indoors or buy young plants. Again, plant out after the last frosts.

Use soil-free compost, place the containers in full sun and water carefully: if the compost is too wet they may rot.

If you are training cordon tomatoes, pinch out the side shoots as they appear. Bush tomatoes and cucumbers should be left to grow naturally, leaving side shoots intact.

The most important things to remember are watering and feeding. Compost should never be allowed to dry out and, once the crops start to develop, a weekly feed of a general purpose liquid or soluble plant fertiliser should be applied to keep the plants growing strongly.

Growing from seed

You can grow vegetables from seed in soil-free compost and there is no need to add a drainage layer. Many vegetables can be sown directly into the compost in spring. You can also sow pinches of seed into small pots or plugs in a cold frame or on a light windowsill for earlier crops.

When they are big enough to handle, thin out the seedlings before moving them into pots. Vegetables in containers can be grown closer together; although the plants may be smaller the yield will be similar.

Cabbages (left) grown in streamlined galvanised metal containers make an elegant display in a more modern garden.

Courgettes (centre) often emerge at the same time as their flowers. They start out small and stripey and mature to a glossier dark green finish.

Tumbling cherry tomatoes (this variety is 'Sweet Million') look pretty partnered by nasturtiums and French marigolds (right). The marigolds will also help to deter aphids.

Salad leaves are a pretty and practical alternative to bedding plants for a summer window box or free-standing trough. Loose-leaf varieties of lettuce with interesting or coloured leaves, either grown alone or mixed with other salad leaves, let you pick a portion at a time without ruining the main display.

To make the planting even more interesting, try adding plants with edible flowers, such as marigolds (*Calendula officinalis*) – particularly the double forms such as 'Fiesta Gitana' – nasturtiums or violas. For the best and quickest results, use a rich compost and feed the plants up to twice a week when they are in full growth.

Making a striking display

In a large tub, even low-growing leaves will make an impact. The main collection here (below) is packed into a plastic trough which resembles an old lead planter.

The seedlings, 'Mira', a red-blushed butterhead lettuce, 'Frisby', a frilly green variety, pale crinkly endive and the smaller leaves of lambs lettuce, were grown in small pots and planted out in the tub when they were still small, positioned for the best display of foliage colour and texture. You c an pack the lettuces in relatively tightly and

then pick off single leaves here and there as you need them for a meal. One sowing should last through summer, provided the leaves are picked regularly to keep the plants bushy.

Other delicious salad leaves

- Summer lettuces include red-leaved 'Redina' and radicchio 'Palla Rossa', frilly red or green-leaved Lollo and green 'Nevada', which is especially crispy.
- Small varieties of lettuce are the best choice for a modest container. Little Gem, a small Cos, and Tom Thumb, a small butterhead lettuce, both grow easily from seed.
- Mixed salad leaves, which combine different flavours, texture and colour, are sold under their own names by many seed companies. They produce leaves but no heart so it is easy to keep snipping a few as and when you need them for a meal.

An edible display (top right) in a window box brings your salad within reach. Plant taller lettuces at the back, small cut and come again leaves in the middle and a pretty nasturtium – which can also be added to the salad – at the front. Or grow lettuce in a pot (below) and harvest it when you need it. A hanging basket just outside the door has an unusual but appealing occupant (below right).

Growing salad on the sill

If you want to bring your salad collection closer to your kitchen scissors, you can grow a variety of plants in a window box, like the vigorous display above.

The box has been planted with the same mixture of salad leaves as the planter opposite, but 'Peach Schnapps', a new variety of edible nasturtium with two-tone flowers, has been added for extra colour and a different taste. It trails attractively over the front and sides, helping to soften the hard edges of the box.

Preparing the box

For the window box shown above, a wrought-iron window-box holder was fixed to the outside wall of the house so that the seedlings could be raised separately.

When the plants were looking good and were ready to enjoy, the terracotta box was dropped into position in the bracket.

Creating the perfect environment

Cushions of springy heather, vivid rhododendrons and sweetly scented azaleas look wonderful, but require very particular soil conditions in order to thrive. The answer is to grow them in containers, giving them the acidic growing conditions that they need to thrive.

Many of our best-loved garden shrubs, such as rhododendrons and azaleas, gaultheria, heathers, kalmia and several heathland berries grow naturally in peaty or boggy locations, particularly in areas with high rainfall, and in soils rich in leaf-mould. All these conditions give soil an acid quality, and such plants will struggle where the soil contains chalk or lime, which are alkaline. Many, including heathers, belong to the family *Ericaceae*, and they are often referred to as ericaceous.

Other garden favourites, such as magnolias, pieris, skimmia and even lupins, will tolerate a little lime but not much, and some shrubs grown for autumn colour, including coryopsis, enkianthus, fothergilla and witch hazel (*Hamamelis*), only produce a really good show if grown in lime-free, humus-rich soil.

Growing acid-lovers in containers

If your garden has chalky, alkaline soil, containers are the perfect way to grow plants that need acidic conditions. Using a lime-free compost is absolutely essential. Most proprietary composts contain some lime, so you must choose one that is labelled as an ericaceous compost. Many of these are largely composed of peat, but if you are concerned about the damage to the environment caused by cutting peat, you should be able to find a compost made with an acid peat substitute.

Ericaceous composts are fine for temporary use, but for a permanent planting their nutrients will soon be exhausted. Instead, use a mixture of two parts (by volume) of moss peat or an acid peat substitute to one part of good, fresh weed-free garden soil. This mixture will suit most acid-loving plants and will sustain good growth for much longer than compost alone.

Watering acid-loving plants

Because tap water is alkaline it will in time have an effect on lime-hating plants. Even if the plant is growing in an acid compost, its leaves will gradually turn yellow, it will cease to thrive and will ultimately die. Ideally, container-grown ericaceous plants should be watered with rainwater or distilled water (such as that produced by dehumidifiers).

If you do not have a water butt, and your only water source is the tap, add a splash of vinegar to the watering can before you dampen your acid-loving plants. You can also water container-grown acid-lovers with a specially formulated ericaceous plant tonic from time to time to give them an added lift.

Compost wisdom

- Check the label on the bag to be sure that its contents are suitable for acid-loving plants (it will probably say 'ericaceous').
- The amount of plant food the compost contains should also be stated. Some have enough food for six weeks, others for six months. Start liquid feeding when compost food runs out.
- Avoid buying bags of compost that have water seeping through the ventilation holes. This indicates they have been stored in wet conditions, which may have caused deterioration.
- Store composts at home in a cool dry place to maintain the balance of nutrients.
- The shelf-life of compost is only about six months. Spread any that is older than this over the garden and buy fresh.

Vibrant pink azaleas (top) tumble in a graceful cascade from a weathered terracotta pot. Using containers allows those with alkaline soil to cultivate their favourite acid-loving plants.

A blue-flowering hydrangea (right) will turn purplish or pink if it is growing in limey soil. Plant one in a pot of ericaceous compost for a wonderful display of clear, sky-blue blooms.

Some plants do best and last longest in alkaline soils rich in lime, and in full sun. If your soil is acid, boggy or shady, you will enjoy more success with the lime-lovers if you grow them in pots. So if you want to grow carnations but don't have the right soil, create the perfect conditions in a container.

Wild, lime-loving plants grow in open, free-draining areas, such as chalk downs or alpine meadows. They include delphiniums, clematis, peonies, stocks and wallflowers, and shrubs like arbutus, broom, buddleja, choisya, daphne, holly and juniper. Many alpine plants and grey or woolly leafed, 'Mediterranean' plants are also lime-lovers, and all can be successfully grown in pots.

Choosing a compost

Plants that will last only one season, like annual dianthus, ornamental kale, wallflowers and ten-week stocks, grow well in general-purpose composts, all of which have lime added during manufacture to balance their acidity. Soil-based compost also contains lime, and will support good growth for the first few months after potting. In permanently planted containers you should always use a soil-based compost – preferably John Innes No.1 or 2 for smaller plants, and John Innes No.3 for established ones.

Topping up

If your tap water is soft, you will also need to apply an annual top dressing of garden lime each spring to permanent plantings: allow 55-115g for each container, depending on its size. Remember that lime is a soil improver, not a plant food, so the container will still need fertiliser. However, you should not mix lime and fertiliser together as this can cause a reaction which will release some of the plant nutrients into the air. To be on the safe side, wait a month after liming before top dressing with fertiliser.

Water with care

Plants that do well in chalky soils can usually tolerate fairly dry conditions. Indeed, they are more likely to be killed by waterlogging than the occasional drying out. Add a good drainage layer to the bottom of your pots and raise them off the ground.

Regular, careful watering to maintain damp, but not soggy, compost is the best policy. Hard water is best for these plants, as it helps to maintain their alkalinity. But if your tap water is soft, or if you use rainwater, which is always soft, for replenishing your soil, the lime will gradually be lost from the compost. In this case you must replace it by adding garden lime to the compost once or twice a year.

Plants that prefer chalky soil

- **Annuals and biennials** alyssum, poppies (*Papaver*), sage (*Salvia*), scabiosa, viola, ornamental cabbage (*Brassica*).
- **Bulbs** anemone, crocus, iris, narcissus, scilla, tulip.
- **Perennials** alyssum, anemone, aubretia, daisies (*Bellis*), campanula, lily of the valley (*Convallaria*), carnations and pinks (*Dianthus*), peony, rudbeckia, saxifrage, verbascum, veronica, yucca.
- **Shrubs** berberis, box (*Buxus*), cotoneaster, daphne, escallonia, hebe, honeysuckle (*Lonicera*), lilac (*Syringa*), olearia, osmanthus, rosemary, viburnum, weigela.

Silver and purple lime-lovers (left) are gathered in harmony. The tiny purple flowers of the hebe and the silvery buds of sage (*Salvia farinacea* 'Strata'), in the smaller pot are echoed by spires of Russian sage (*Perovskia* 'Blue Spire') and silver sea holly in the larger one.

A small pot of pinks (below left) will add the heady scent of cloves to your patio. All they need is the slightly alkaline compost they prefer.

Sunny wallflowers (below right) make perfect companions to many spring bulbs. Although tolerant of most soils, they prefer a little lime.

A clematis (opposite) may grow better in a container, where you can give it limey soil.

Some of the most delightful plants need cool moist conditions if they are to thrive. And luckily you don't have to live near a bog to enjoy their beauty – you can create a scaled-down damp patch, miniature bog garden or river bank quite easily in a container.

When your natural garden conditions are hot, dry or free draining, you can still provide the conditions that many moisture-lovers, such as filipendula and ranunculus, prefer in a container. To get the best out of moisture-loving plants, start by using the biggest container you have room for, as this will stay damp longer and will not need constant watering. Bog plants, like marsh marigolds (*Caltha*) and gunnera, look particularly good in large half-barrels; otherwise choose any container that will retain moisture well.

A compost that holds moisture

Most moisture-loving plants will grow perfectly well in a good-quality, soil-free compost, as long as it does not dry out. But soil-based composts will retain moisture longer between waterings, especially if you add water-retaining granules to the compost before planting up.

Maintaining moisture levels

For moisture-loving plants, free drainage is not particularly desirable, provided that water does not stand in the container indefinitely. This means that you do not need to put a layer of drainage material in the base, although it is still a good idea to stand the tub on bricks or similar supports so that the holes in the base do not become blocked up.

Because moisture-lovers soon lose condition – the leaves wilt and turn brown and the plants die quickly if they become dry, even for a short

while – automatic watering is ideal. It means they will never dry out accidentally and will still cope unsupervised during a wet spell – when other plants may be drowned.

Selecting a shady spot

Most moisture-loving plants also prefer shady or partially shaded conditions so try, if you can, to stand the container under a tree or in the shadow of a wall. And you can help to keep your plants in tip-top condition by adding a liquid feed to the watering can weekly or fortnightly during summer.

Moisture-loving plants

If you want to grow plants that prefer damp and shade you could opt for a bold effect with just one giant gunnera or *Rheum* (resembling huge rhubarb) or *Rodgersia* (like a large filipendula), or you can choose from these groups:

- **Grasses and grass-like plants**, such as Bowles' golden grass, (*Carex* 'Evergold'), miniature bulrush and sweet flag (*Acorus calamus*), or the bamboo-like *Arundinaria viridistriata*.
- **Moisture-loving flowering perennials** such as giant cowslip (*Primula florindae*), globeflowers (*Trollius*), hemp agrimony (*Eupatorium cannabinum*) and purple loosestrife (*Lythrum salicaria*) will give the impression of a pond margin.
- Box elder, dogwood (*Cornus*), ornamental elders (*Sambucus*) and willows (*Salix*), prefer moisture and can be grown in pots.

Bamboos like to get their feet wet: here it is growing with another moisture-lover, gunnera.

Purple irises, the beardless variety *Iris sibirica* 'Shirley Pope', and shuttlecock ferns will both grow best in damp and shady conditions.

Plants from hot countries like Australia, Mexico and South Africa, are able to withstand drought and continuous heat, so they make carefree choices for sun-baked containers. Sun-loving annuals will grow profusely throughout summer if they are positioned to catch the light at its brightest.

Choose the largest pot possible. Even drought-loving plants will need watering two or three times a day if planted in tiny pots. Only pelargoniums and nasturtiums, will flower more profusely in the stressed conditions of a small pot.

Succulents and tropicals

Fat-leaved succulents such as echeveria, and many of the euphorbia and sedum families, revel in hot sun and dry compost by storing water in their leaves. And plants with narrow, spiky foliage, including yuccas and many tropical palms and grasses, retain their own moisture well.

Aromatics

Mediterranean plants which have pale grey aromatic foliage, including helichrysum, lavenders, rosemary and santolina, are perfectly adapted to long periods of scorching sun and drought as they have a high level of oil in their leaves, which reduces water loss. A standard bay tree looks good with a culinary underplanting of thyme and both plants prefer a light, well-drained chalky soil and a sunny position.

Decorative mulches

To give plants their best chance of survival, reduce the amount of water lost from the pot by topping it with a thick layer of mulch such as pebbles, crushed recycled glass, the colour of green and amber rough-cut semi-precious stones, will enhance the subtle colours and rosette shapes of sempervivum.

Shade for summer

Provide shade with a vertical planting of fast-growing climbers, supported by a twiggy or metal obelisk, or trained around a pergola. Morning glory, climbing nasturtiums, passionflowers, sweet peas and the Chilean glory vine (*Eccremocarpus*) will romp away in hot, dry conditions.

Or, you can make the most of spring sunshine by selecting climbers such as wisteria, which produces chandeliers of fragrant flowers followed by dense summer foliage. Or choose fragrant summer flowering shrubs, such as clerodendron and many of the viburnum family, which will reflect the waning sunlight later in the year and produce bright autumn fruits.

Sun-loving plants

These plants will thrive in the scorching heat.

- **Annuals** *Cosmos bipinnatus*, *gazania*, morning glory, opium poppy (*Papaver somniferum*), nasturtium (*Tropaeolum majus*)
- **Bedding and patio plants** *Bidens*, *Diascia*, *Helichrysum petiolare*, marguerite (*Argyranthemum*), *Portulaca grandiflora*, *Senecio cineraria*, tobacco plant (*Nicotiana*), zinnia

Bougainvillea (top left) is a classic Mediterranean plant. A gravel mulch cuts water loss.

Shades of gold from dahlias, (near left) french marigolds and rudbeckia mingle with whirligig heads of osteospermum.

Cool colours shimmer in hot settings (right). The lavenders give the impression of a traditional bed bordering a path, while the silver pots and foliage echo the sun-bleached wood.

Alpines in containers

Originally from high mountain and dry desert regions, alpines and succulents actually grow most successfully in poor soils. Pots are the perfect way to provide these typical rockery plants with conditions that suit them, and will also help to draw attention to their often tiny features.

Under normal garden conditions, where the soil has been improved and fed over the years, alpines and succulents grow tall and lanky, flower poorly and die early. But with low soil fertility and free drainage, they grow strong and stocky, with abundant flowers. Perennials, such as pinks (*Dianthus),* aubretia, candytuft, gentian and saxifrage, will live to a ripe old age.

Mimicking natural conditions

In their natural habitat, alpines root in rock crevices or pockets of gritty soil, so in pots most prefer a coarse compost, that holds a certain amount of moisture. Succulents, such as lampranthus and sedums, often grow in little more than rocky debris in the wild. Sempervivums or houseleeks, will even grow 'planted' between the tiles of a leaking roof where they spread to plug the hole.

Alpines do not need deep soil or compost, so sinks, seed pans, shallow troughs and similar make ideal containers. Whatever pot you use, it must be free draining, so be sure to make plenty of holes and place a good layer of drainage material in the base.

Mulch for protection

The leaves of many alpines will go brown and rot if they touch wet compost, so it is a good idea to cover the surface with a 2.5cm mulch of coarse grit, granite chippings or gravel. Including a few large craggy stones in the arrangement will add to the alpine effect. You could even plant a sempervivum in a stone with a hole in it, or in an empty shell for a seaside theme.

Preparing for planting

Fill the container with a proprietary alpine compost. This will contain a mixture of loam, peat or peat substitute and sharp sand, or grit, to ensure that the plants' roots do not become waterlogged, plus just enough fertiliser to get the plants off to a good start. Alternatively, you can make your own mix of one part topsoil, one part sieved leaf-mould or peat substitute, and one part grit or fine pea shingle.

Most alpines are not drought tolerant, but equally they hate to be waterlogged. So the compost must be kept reasonably damp, particularly during the growing season.

Feed for success

For really healthy alpines and succulents, give your plants a weak liquid feed at the beginning of the growing season. Choose a feed with a fertiliser that is suitable for flowering plants, but avoid one that contains a high level of nitrogen, as this will encourage the plants to grow up tall, weak and with a straggly appearance.

Poor soil in a natural environment

The tough conditions that suit alpines are also perfect for many of Britain's native wild flowers, which thrive on roadside verges.

- **Bring the countryside to your patio**, and attract beneficial insects, by growing plants like baby blue eyes (*Nemophila*), love-in-a-mist (*Nigella damascena*), and poached egg flower (*Limnanthes douglasii*).
- **Don't use multipurpose compost** or your wild flowers will grow leggy with lots of foliage, but few blooms. Use an alpine mix instead and keep feeding to a minimum, and you will be rewarded with sturdy plants and a profusion of flowers.

A seaside flower which dislikes the cold and wet, but flourishes in dry conditions, *Asteriscus* (right) grows as an annual in a basket of free-draining compost.

Top a tall slender glazed pot with a crown of sculptural houseleeks (far right). Their pink-tinged rosettes will glow like a flaming torch.

A collection of little terracotta 'long Toms' containing succulents, sempervivums and alpines are gathered together in an antique wire bottle holder to make an appealingly casual display. They would be equally at home in a conservatory.

It is a common misconception that only foliage plants will thrive in shade. In fact, a wealth of flowering varieties prefer a cool and sheltered spot out of the glare of direct sunlight. Woodland plants are a natural choice for a shady position, since they have evolved to survive beneath the tree canopy.

When you want to grow plants to add interest to the area beneath a tree, using containers often gives better results than planting into the ground, where the new plants have to compete with the tree for water and nutrients.

If your patio is sheltered by a deciduous tree or large shrub, spring varieties, such as crocuses, daffodils and primroses will do well in the dappled light that filters through before the dense covering of new leaves has formed. When the branches are bare again in autumn the spot will be perfect for colchicum, cyclamen, hellebores and Japanese anemones.

Shady summer plants

Summer-flowering plants that can cope with a lack of light are harder to find, but the herbaceous perennial geranium known as cranesbill is a versatile choice. It grows in a range of habits from prostrate and spreading to upright and clump-forming and with a choice of colours including pinks and reds, blues and purples and shades of white.

Geranium phaeum has exquisite dark purple flowers but can tolerate the deepest shade unlike the newer annual zonal pelargoniums which need full sun.

Planting near a seating area

A shady corner is the obvious place to create a seating area. Busy lizzies and fuchsias give bright colour in gloomy surroundings. Choose varieties with white flowers to fill the space with a luminous glow at twilight.

Many white-flowering plants have a delicious scent that is strongest in the late afternoon or early evening, when they attract pollinating nocturnal insects. Tobacco plants and lilies both thrive in pots.

Catching the light

Many large-leaved plants can tolerate shade because their wide surface area makes the most of the available light. Hostas are a typical example, and are particularly well-suited to being grown in containers, where their juicy leaves can be more easily protected from slugs and snails.

A collection of foliage plants with contrasting textures will make a striking display. Try combining broad-leaved hostas with the delicate filigree shapes of lush ferns or the arching stems of a bamboo. All these plants will grow happily in shady spots provided they are never allowed to dry out.

If there is space for a really large container placed near a tree or a shaded wall you can provide support for a climbing hydrangea or one of the many evergreen ivies whose mottled white, gold or cream leaves will lighten the darkest corner. Many variegated shrubs will revert to plain green if deprived of sunlight for a long time, but ivies retain their interest.

Great plants for shady places

- **Annuals** busy lizzies; lobelia; mimulus
- **Bulbs** Allium hollandicum 'Purple Sensation'; cyclamen; lilies; snowflake (Leucojum)
- **Flowering plants** astilbe; buttercup or crowfoot (Ranunculus lyallii); escallonia; phlox (woodland perennial varieties); Solomon's seal (Polygonatum)
- **Foliage plants** fatsia; heuchera; hoheria; hosta; ivy; Japanese painted fern (Athyrium niponicum); lungwort (Pulmonaria); spotted laurel (Aucuba japonica 'Variegata'); stripy bulbous oat grass (Arrhenatherum elatius ssp. bulbosum); variegated ground elder

In a shady border, creamy yellow petunias and a pale-edged hosta (top left) glow in a matching 'big-top' striped barrel. They illuminate and draw attention to the ferns and alchemilla mollis growing there.

Nodding spires of pink foxgloves tower above a bed of shuttlecock ferns (*Matteuccia struthiopteris*) (left). A fallen log in the garden inspired this woodland arrangement of shade and moisture-loving plants.

A green fountain of fern fronds (below) spurts from an old drainpipe hopper, lifting an otherwise dark corner.

Containers for every season

Spring bulbs

Bright, fresh-flowering tubs bursting with exuberant blooms chime with the sense of renewal that comes with the warmer weather and lengthening days that herald the coming of spring.

Greet the arrival of springtime with a glorious display of sunny, yellow narcissi and creamy white hyacinths. Bulbs prefer a well-drained, moderately fertile soil that is kept moist but never waterlogged. So ensure your container has lots of drainage holes and is lined with plenty of crocks.

The pretty pale daffodil 'Ice Follies' (below) produces creamy white petals around a pale primrose cup, which turns white as the flower matures. At around 38cm tall, these form the focal point of the display. Depending on the size of the container, arrange five, seven or nine bulbs in the centre (odd numbers look more natural than even numbers). If you prefer a scented variety, choose 'Cheerfulness', or the newer 'Martinette', which is slightly shorter.

Mix varieties that flower at the same time as one another. A circle of smaller daffodils, *Narcissus* 'Hawera' has been placed around the central group. They grow just 20cm tall and bear from two to six lightly fragrant, canary-yellow flowers on each stem. Finally, dot several white or cream hyacinths in among the smaller narcissi.

A natural effect

The multiflora hyacinths used here are closer in character to the wild species than many other cultivated varieties and produce stems of loosely arranged flowers to create a very natural effect. As hyacinth bulbs are more expensive than narcissi, save money by planting them only in the front half of the container. This display was planted in a traditional wooden half-barrel painted with

Make a cheerful statement (left) on a front doorstep with this white tub brimming with daffodils and hyacinths. The varieties have been chosen for their colour and scent.

Colour holds a group together (right) as the miniature daffodils are linked to the larger ones through the golden eyes of the polyanthus, and the pink and mauve of the two polyanthus echo with the magnolia blossom in the background.

Extending the season

Have a longer display in the same pot by starting it off at the turn of the year with early blooming bulbs.

- **Winter** Dwarf narcissus and a creamy white anemone blanda flower in winter. While these bloom, the buds of the later daffodils will begin to push through the foliage, ready to take over where the early flowers leave off.
- **Spring** The arrangement will look as it does on the left.

winter

spring

two coats of weatherproof paint. White paint helps pale petals to make an impact, where a stronger colour could overpower them. If the half-barrel is to be a permanent feature by a front door, say – choose a colour that coordinates with the paintwork.

Hints and tips for beautiful bulbs

- **Buying** Most bulbs sold in autumn are foolproof. If you buy them in advance, keep them in a cool place. Choose bulbs that have no visible shoots and whose outer skin, or tunic, is intact. Avoid bulbs kept in a warm place, where they may have been sweating in their plastic bags.
- **Planting** Plant daffodils by September so that they develop a strong root system. For a good display, plant the bulbs very close together, or even touching. The golden rule for a generous effect is to fill the container – don't leave any gaps because the finished result will be less attractive. Daffodil bulbs should be planted at a depth of approximately twice their own height, with their pointed noses uppermost.
- **Compost** Use John Innes No.1 with a little multipurpose feed and a few handfuls of grit.
- **Watering** You are unlikely to drown your bulbs as any surplus moisture will drain away.

56 Polyanthus

The cheerful blotched faces of polyanthus and primulas have an old-fashioned, fresh-from-the-country look, but they can hold their own in today's smart containers too.

Early in the year, polyanthus and primulas bring a splash of vivid colour to the garden at a time when it is usually quite dull. Both flowers belong to the same family, but spotting the difference between them is quite easy: polyanthus flowers emerge in clusters of colour at the end of flower stalks whereas primulas all flower from the centre of the plant.

It is essential when using small plants like polyanthus to think about how to provide drama and interest.

Choosing a suitable container

Start with the pot and choose one that suits the location: a shiny galvanised metal container on decking, for example, or warm terracotta pots for an elegant tiled doorstep. Then select your polyanthus in colours that complement both the container and location.

One way to highlight low-growing plants like polyanthus is to add a focal plant to the group to give it emphasis and to bring out the colour of the smaller specimens. Raising the pot on a table or bench can also give a modest polyanthus much-needed height.

Growing tips

You can buy young plants of polyanthus and primroses from a garden centre or grow them from seed sown in early spring. They can be packed quite tightly together for a profuse display, but in that case you must use a deep container so that the roots can grow down into the compost. If crammed into a shallow bowl without sufficient space for the roots to spread down or sideways, polyanthus will last only two or three weeks. Dead-head the plants regularly and they will flower all spring.

For a pale and pretty pot team yellow polyanthus with creamy primroses and *Primula denticulata* var. 'Alba'. Spiky liriope, ivy and woolly grey senecio add texture.

Cool colours shine in metal containers, as these primroses show (left). Behind, cream-flowered hellebores add height and the grouping gains added style through repetition.

Key facts

- The progeny of wild meadow cowslips and primroses, polyanthus are robust plants, hardy to −15°C. The flowers can be single, double or hose-in-hose, in which there are two rows of petals one inside the other.
- **Barnhaven** varieties often have speckled flowers held high above the foliage.
- **Gold-laced** polyanthus have single-petalled blooms with golden eyes and a gold edge to a second colour.
- **Charisma Series** are large and bi-coloured, with a golden centre.
- **Gemini Series** have single-coloured or two-tone flowers with a yellow centre.

The waving grass, *Carex* 'Evergold', (right) draws the eye to the warm pink *Primula* 'Betty', set in an antique reclaimed container. Placing the arrangement on a table lifts it to a more comfortable eye-level height.

Mix the foliage to give structure to a planting. Balls of the 'Red Baron' polyanthus (left) are backed by the shapely leaves of *Helleborus orientalis guttatus* and fringed with 'Golden Inge' ivy.

Holding their heads erect, tulips look great in a pot, on their own or with other spring bulbs. Available in a huge range of colours and sizes, plain and striped, smooth and frilled, whether open or shut, their curves and colours always look magnificent.

The passion for tulips dates back hundreds of years. When 'tulipomania' swept through Holland in the 17th century, a single bulb could cost the equivalent of a house in Amsterdam.

Tulips make a fabulous display, densely planted in containers. The Greigii variety used in these arrangements is a late-flowering tulip, bringing colour when most spring bulbs have finished. It has stunning flowers, often bi-coloured and beautiful leaves, mottled or striped with crimson.

In the arrangement below right, 'Plaisir' tulip, a carmine-red bloom with yellow edges, and 'Treasure', a softer pinky red with creamy edges are teamed with 'Delft Blue' hyacinths. The hyacinth's heavily scented clear blue flowers can be grown to coincide with the blooms of the tulips.

If you prefer to focus solely on the impact of these unusual tulips, they can be planted on their own (below). Packed together, the stems hold the blooms upright while the leaves curl prettily over the edge of the pot.

Growing tulips

- **Pack bulbs tightly** into the container so that they touch. You don't have to leave room for the bulbs to spread.
- **Support taller varieties** by growing something wiry like a winter heather around the tulips.
- **When flowering is finished,** move the bulbs into the garden – they are not as good a second time round. Use fresh bulbs next year.

A carefully chosen pot can be the making of a display. The fluted edges of this terracotta planter echo the curvaceous shape of the tulip leaves, while the glazed pattern traced on the pot's surface complements the distinctive mottled stripes of the foliage.

Extending the season

Different varieties of tulip bloom at different times so you can keep a container going for months by mixing them. Choose three colours that will look good together as buds and flowers. Here the colours gradually become more intense.

- **Early spring** White 'Diana' tulips flower first.
- **Mid spring** The pink-edged 'Garden Party' comes through.
- **Late spring** Finish with deep maroon 'Queen of the Night'.

early
spring

mid
spring

late
spring

With their slightly unkempt cottage garden look, loosely rambling petunias add a brilliant or delicate note to summer schemes and mingle easily with a variety of other plants.

Plain or striped, veined or frilly, upright or trailing, single or double, the trumpet-shaped flowers of petunias will fill a pot or hanging basket with a mass of dependable colour from midsummer to the first winter frosts.

Petunias originally came in strong and dominant colours: white, cream, pink, red, mauve and blue. But some of the newest strains have single flowers in gentle pastel shades that suit more restrained arrangements.

A brighter container

In the simple grouping (far right), the white and lime-green stripes of the half-barrel are the brightest colours in the arrangement. The colours of the plants are intentionally and subtly low-key, although when the hosta flowers, its lilac-blue spire will add welcome height to the display.

After the petunias have died down, the hosta could be underplanted with yellow winter pansies. These could be replaced the following spring with primroses to keep the creamy colour scheme going.

Growing tips

For containers it is simpler to buy young petunias. Plant them in multipurpose compost and give them plenty of drainage. They can stand full sun and benefit from a liquid feed every two weeks once they start flowering. Keep dead-heading to encourage more flowers.

Key facts

Most of today's petunias are derived from F1 hybrids:

- **The Multiflora Group** grows to around 30cm, is vigorous, large flowered and tolerant of poor weather. 'Delight', 'Carpet' and 'Duo' are semi-double, while 'Mirage' has the largest flowers. The Surfinia Series flowers extra vigorously.
- **The Grandiflora Group,** including the 'Cloud', 'Pirouette' and 'Super Cascade' Series, has the largest flowers, but is not as bushy as the Multifloras and is less resilient to wet weather.
- **The Milliflora Group** includes 'Million Bells' and 'Carillion', which produce masses of small flowers and are especially suitable to use in hanging baskets.

In a shady spot, the eye is drawn by the vertical stripes of the barrel, echoed in the stripy leaves of the hosta (right). The muted flowers of *Petunia* 'Cascade Yellow Eye', a new variety, add a more restful note.

A dramatic setting shows off the brilliant trailing petunia 'Surfinia Pink Vein' (below). Here the striped *Yucca flaccida* 'Golden Sword' is centre stage, framed by petunias and the delicate flowers of *Nemesia* 'Confetti'. Orange gerberas, placed either side like spotlights, draw the eye to the display.

Matching blue-glazed pots of petunias tucked into the side of a miniature waterfall seem almost to be growing wild (left). The larger container is packed with mixed purple and white flowers, the smaller one has a simpler planting of plain white.

The sweet-smelling perfume of roses and other fragrant flowers wafting gently on a summer breeze is a delight. Reap a sensual feast with these glorious high-season container ideas.

Nothing proclaims summer better than the wonderful fragrance of flowers. Container gardeners do not have to miss out on the delightful scent of roses: while patio varieties are the obvious choice for growing in pots, the more blowzy and heavily scented border varieties will do just as well if you meet their needs. All shrub roses like to put out deep roots, so make sure that your container is at least 60cm tall and that it is filled with a good rich compost.

Glorious musk roses

For a sweet scent, choose any of the hybrid musk roses, with their long, graceful growth and delicate colours. 'Felicia' is one of the finest examples, a compact, bushy grower with silvery pink flowers, which bloom

Extending the season

- **Early summer** A pot of stocks (*Matthiola*) in soft purples and pinks will give fragrance from late spring into summer. Team them with a small pot of white freesias.
- **Midsummer** Plant the main arrangement of petunias, roses and nicotianas on the right.
- **Late summer** Remove the nicotianas and the rose as they fade and replace them with a white gardenia – a deliciously scented evergreen shrub. Repeat the colour theme with a small pot of pink and white dianthus.

early summer

midsummer

late summer

early summer

midsummer

late summer

profusely in early summer then at intervals until autumn, and dark, shiny leaves.

Purple *Petunia* 'Priscilla' and pale pink scented tobacco plants (*Nicotiana* Domino Series) surround the base of the rose and fill a smaller separate pot. They will provide colour and scent throughout summer, when the rose is at its best. Lift them out when flowering has finished and move the main pot to a less prominent spot within the garden until the rose is ready to bloom again next summer. Prune the rose carefully in winter by taking off half the previous season's growth to retain its bushy shape.

Indulge your senses

Make the most of a secluded corner by surrounding a seat with scented plants to create a pleasant retreat for a balmy afternoon, when the flowers' perfume will be most distinct.

The alternative arrangement (far left) teams a tall pot of 'Journey's End' lilies with a shallow bowl filled with other fragrant plants. Three varieties of alpine pinks, or *Dianthus* – 'Brilliant Star' (white), 'India Star' (ruby red) and 'Pixie Star' (lavender pink) – blend their sweet scent with the aroma of variegated 'Silver Posie' thyme.

Clashing reds and pinks make a hot summer display (far left). A striking red seat picks out the common colour of the ruby-veined, pink-speckled 'Journey's End' lilies and the mixture of alpine pinks.

Velvety purple petunias accent the paler tones of a 'Felicia' musk rose, blush pink nicotianas and their ornate pinky terracotta pot. The enchanting miniature version without the rose, planted in a seed pan, reinforces the theme.

64 Geraniums

With a flowering season that stretches for months, happily tolerant of being allowed to dry out and with a vast range of varieties to choose from, the geranium is deservedly the king of container plants.

Geraniums epitomise the atmosphere of summer holidays in Italy and Greece with hot sun and blue skies. Even in a cooler climate, their scarlet ranks (below) create the illusion of sunshine. The simplicity of the planting – 60 identical plants in plastic pots – works perfectly against the plain white wall. Because it reflects the sun that they love, white is the perfect background for geraniums; they never stand out as well against red brick.

Geraniums in softer tones

Bright red geraniums are the choice for a Mediterranean look, but in the muted light of a northern summer, quieter tones can be as attractive.

The softer arrangement (far right) is a reminder that hanging baskets do not always have to be attached to a wall. The silver bucket and chain makes an

unexpected but harmonious contrast to the pale bark of the Worcester Pearmain apple tree, and the pastel flowers blend softly into the summer foliage.

To mix geraniums with other plants, stay with shades of a single colour: mix a mauve flowered geranium with purple verbena. Or try a red geranium with mimulus and red lobelia for a dramatic effect.

Growing tips

Geraniums thrive in direct sun so choose their planting partners with care: trailing lobelia for example needs regular watering and will suffer in the dry conditions that geraniums love. Deadhead geraniums regularly and pull off dead leaves.

Geraniums are not really hardy plants, but they can be overwintered outdoors in a sheltered city garden. Here they will harden off and flower even better the next year.

A touch of the Mediterranean is easy to conjure up using ranks of red geraniums on a whitewashed wall (left).

A simple way to group pots is to gather them into one container (right). It works particularly well if you can find one as pretty as this old milk crate, loaded with 'Tip Top' geraniums.

A stylish bucket of ivy-leaved geraniums bridges the seasons (far right). The white flowers recall the apple blossom of spring while the pink ones draw the eye to the ripening apples behind.

Key facts

Geraniums (*Pelargoniums*) are strongly formed plants, some more upright than others, which bloom with double or single flowers.

- **Zonal pelargoniums** are bushy and upright, with horseshoe-shaped markings on the leaves and single and double flowers.

- **Regal pelargoniums** have enormous flowers, with or without petal markings, and are usually single. They grow to 46cm and are suited to large containers.

- **Ivy-leaved pelargoniums** have single or double flowers. This trailing form is ideal for hanging baskets and edging containers.

- **Scented-leaved pelargoniums** are typically grown for their aromatic leaves, which vary in size and shape, they usually have small, single pale pink flowers.

- **Angel pelargoniums**, sometimes known as 'Tip Top', are dense plants with delicate two-tone flowers.

Reflect the cycle of the seasons in a single container by choosing just one kind of hardy shrub or evergreen as a permanent backbone for your pot, and planting colourful variations around it throughout the year.

Simply by planning ahead you can keep a single container looking its colourful best all year long. With a permanent plant as the basis of your scheme, a succession of seasonal variations will add fresh interest as the months go by.

Choosing the right pot is important if you want an arrangement to last all year. It needs to be frost-proof and should have plenty of space for the roots of the permanent plant to spread.

Start in summer

French lavender (*Lavandula stoechas*) is the backbone of the main arrangement on the right and will remain in the pot all year round. Its dense flowerheads are a deep purple, with rosy purple bracts perching like butterflies at their tips. Surround the fragrant stems with pretty blooms in toning colours by adding a miniature pink rose in front of the lavender and purple violas around the edge.

As the seasons change, you can alter the planting (top right). Vary the colours of the seasonal plants to complement the lavender as it shifts from its regal purple when in bloom to the silvery foliage later in the year.

Include a slow-release fertiliser when you first plant up the container and add a little fresh compost each time you change or add to the arrangement.

Focus on the front of the pot, and away from the pruned lavender, by planting low-growing crocus and foliage (left). Nestle a few pine cones in the display for a wintry effect.

Pick out the purple of the French lavender with a frilly collar of matching violas (right). Miniature pink roses provide substance to the arrangement and echo the rotund shape of the big-bellied pot.

Extending the season

- **Summer** Plant lavender and pink roses in the centre of the pot and purple violas at the front.
- **Autumn** Replace the roses and violas with rosy pink and white ornamental cabbages.
- **Winter** Prune the lavender, remove the cabbages and add silvery plants to highlight the lavender foliage: pale lilac crocus, silvery *Senecio cineraria* and variegated ivies.
- **Spring** Return to a darker purple as the lavender buds begin to show, by filling the space in front of the shrub with *Iris reticulata*.

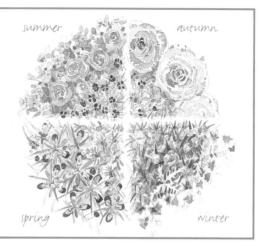

68 Busy lizzies

For colour that will glow all summer long, even on the gloomiest basement patio and prove resistant to most insect invaders, no plant is so rewarding – and so foolproof – as a simple busy lizzie.

Busy lizzies (*Impatiens*) are often under-rated perhaps because of their ubiquity in hanging baskets and local parks, where they are chosen because they are so easy to grow. But they make good-natured, long-lasting container plants, and thrive in shade: a pot of white busy lizzies will create a pool of light in the darkest corner. Just consider grouping and texture as you plant them and you can enjoy their many good qualities.

Grouping bizzy lizzies

If you want to arrange busy lizzies in a group, use three different sizes of matching containers and go from pale to bright, drawing the eye to a dramatic climax in the largest pot. In the arrangement (below right) the pots are stepped up in size like building blocks, with the smallest planted with pale pink flowers, the medium pot with lilac and the largest with a strong coral red.

A ring of colour

Another way of using busy lizzies is to make them the frame for a focal point, such as a group of lilies. A good starting point is to find a container that catches your eye in the garden centre and to decide where you will put it. You can then wheel it around the centre while you select the plants that will suit the pot and the position.

Lighting can transform a simple container arrangement of a single variety of busy lizzies into something special. This candleholder is an old Christmas decoration, recycled to add a 'table setting' feel to an outside display.

The arrangement (below right) shows the dark green glaze of the pot mirrored in three shades and textures of foliage. Four pink-centred white-flowered *Impatiens* 'New Guinea', alternate with four *Alchemilla mollis* with velvety foliage. They make a wonderful setting for the centrepiece of 'Casa Blanca' lilies, whose spiky leaves add yet another variation of foliage.

Growing tips

Plant busy lizzies in well-drained multi-purpose compost in spring after the risk of frost has passed. Pack lots of plants into the container for maximum effect.

Busy lizzies prefer dappled sunshine to full sun and will flower reliably in shade. Pinch out the tips of the young plants to encourage them to bush up. Water regularly and give a weekly liquid feed. Deadhead busy lizzies frequently and they will continue to flower into autumn.

Key facts

Impatiens are sold mostly as annual bedding plants, although there is a shrubby form known as *Impatiens* 'New Guinea' (below).

- **The 'Super Elfin' Series** of *Impatiens walleriana* are low growing, but can also be used as trailers. The Tempo, Swirl and Accent Series all derive from this species and the colours range from pastels to shades of pink, orange and violet.
- **New Guinea Impatiens** have larger leaves, with mainly single flowers but there is a double form known as 'Double Impatiens'. Colours include rose, salmon, lavender, white and many bi-colours; 'Spectra' also has variegated leaves.
- **Dwarf cultivars**, such as *Impatiens balsamina* 'Tom Thumb' grow to just 30cm, with big double flowers in white, pink, scarlet and violet.

A mixed group of pink busy lizzies and purple lobelia brings a refreshing cottage garden look to a formal setting (centre left). Their relaxed shapes soften the firmer, formal outlines of the tiered box ball, bamboos, ferns and acanthus.

Pots of busy lizzies make bold brush strokes of colour in the shade of a large shrub (near left). By keeping the planting simple, the vibrant combination of pink, lilac and coral works well. It is underplanted with trailing *Sutera* (*Bacopa*) 'Snowflake' for added texture and interest.

For interesting combinations look outside the usual container plants (right). Here a border perennial, *Alchemilla mollis*, rubs shoulders with elegant lilies and modest busy lizzies to make a display that will bloom happily in shady conditions.

70 Autumn warmth

Take your cues from the trees and fill your autumn containers with rich shades of russet and bronze. As the temperature starts to fall, these fiery colours will add a glow to any garden.

Chrysanthemums are available all year round, but they are at their best in autumn, when the pot-grown dwarf plants make a glorious container display for six to eight weeks.

In the main arrangement (right), pink, purple and deep red chrysanthemums with daisy-like flowerheads throng the edge of a large pale stone container, interspersed with a few hardy plumbago plants (*Ceratostigma plumbaginoides*), shrubby perennials that bear clusters of tiny bright blue flowers in late summer and whose leaves turn an attractive red in autumn.

In the centre of the large pot is a smaller pot, planted with *Heuchera* 'Chocolate Ruffles'. The deep purply red foliage is a striking focal point and emphasises the rich and luxurious colour scheme. After the chrysanthemums have flowered, they could be replaced with a deep pink cyclamen, without disturbing the heuchera (see box on opposite page).

Warm colour, sweet scent

For a glowing alternative to the purples of the main display, choose burnt oranges, yellows and deep bronzes (below). Double daisy-shaped chrysanthemums massed in a glazed pot give fiery colour. Perfume is always a welcome addition to any planting and a variety of wallflower (*Erysimum* Aida Series) planted with them has strongly scented flowers in autumn and again in spring. Remove the seed heads as they form to prolong the flowering.

Chrysanthemum plants are best bought in flower or with fat, coloured buds, just ready to burst. Immature green buds may not open.

A deep mustard glazed pot (left) echoes the rich bronzes of autumn flowers and leaves. Stand this display where it will pick up the colours of a tree or add interest to a dull spot.

Lookalikes

The chrysanthemum name encompasses a wide range of different flowers from large, top-heavy blowzy pompoms, through shaggier varieties to the daintiest daisy-like blooms. If you want alternative summer daisy style flowers for this display, try one of these species: *Argyranthemum* (Marguerite daisies); *Dendranthema*; *Leucanthemum* or *Leucanthemopsis* (Moon daisies).

Extending the season

Evergreen heucheras flower in summer. Vary the plantings in the outer pot to complement the attractive purple leaves of the heuchera throughout the year.

- **Summer** Fill the larger pot with sweet williams (*Dianthus barbatus*) in reds and pinks.
- **Autumn** Replace the sweet williams, with similarly-toned chrysanthemums and the bright blues of plumbago.
- **Winter** Take out the hardy plumbago and chrysanthemums and replace them with white and pink heathers for winter colour.

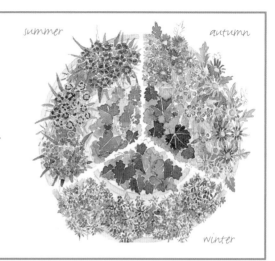

summer   autumn   winter

Stacking pots adds height to an arrangement of short plants and allows you to mix species that need different composts. Choose pots from the same family and put an upside-down flowerpot in the lower container to support the inner one.

Capture the spirit of autumn with a colourful harvest of decorative fruit and vegetables. Choose inedible varieties you won't be tempted to pick, and enjoy this display on misty October and November days.

Shiny scarlet and orange peppers and gorgeous crinkly purple cabbages make an exotic take on the traditional harvest festival basket (main picture, right). The pepper used is *Capsicum annuum*, the ornamental pepper. These are, in fact, edible (although not necessarily tasty), but be sure not to confuse this pepper with *Solanum pseudocapsicum* whose fruits are extremely poisonous.

Colours and shapes

Ornamental peppers vary greatly in colour and shape. You can choose from the long, slender tapering red hot chilli peppers and the wider, cone-shaped peppers used here, which are white or green when immature and will eventually turn to a brilliant scarlet or purple.

Gathering the fruits

In the arrangement (right) the bare branches of late autumn trees are echoed by a rustic planter – a loosely woven twiggy basket – which adds to the sense of a newly gathered autumn harvest. The basket has been lined with dyed sisal fibre, a longer-lasting and more environmentally friendly choice than moss. Plant the cabbages and peppers closely for maximum impact and to help retain moisture: this is a planting that needs to be kept well watered.

A visual autumn feast can be as bright as any summer collection. For the best display choose pepper plants with fully formed fruits (left); they will last for between four and six weeks, or until the first frost.

Heathers and pernettya thrive in acid compost while the peppers do not. So the peppers were sunk into the display while still encapsulated in their own pots (right), each filled with the standard compost they prefer.

In frost-prone areas, the basket should be kept raised above ground level and placed in a sheltered spot – perhaps close to a back door or under a kitchen window. All the plants used here are annuals and are best discarded after two or three months or as soon as frost strikes.

A splash of red

In the alternative arrangement (below left), ornamental peppers add warmth and brilliance to a pair of green glazed pots filled with the perennial evergreens *Erica gracilis* and *Gaultheria mucronata*.

The pink sheen of the gaultheria berries, the glossy peppers and the oily blue-green glaze on the pots all work together to give a superbly rich effect. You can leave the peppers in their individual pots and sink them into the compost: the rims will be completely hidden. Once the peppers fade, they can be removed, leaving small empty pots in which you can plant winter pansies or spring bulbs to keep the container going for as long as the heather looks good.

The heather, *Erica gracilis*, or 'Cape Heath', is a compact bushy plant with tiny urn-shaped flowers that appear in autumn and continue flourishing through to spring. *Gaultheria mucronata* needs to be planted in groups to ensure plenty of cross-pollination, if it is to produce its eye-catching masses of white, pink, red or mulberry-purple berries.

Winter pansies

Simple and sweet, with their vibrant colours, velvet texture and upturned faces, pansies brighten even the dreariest winter days. Despite their small size, they are endlessly versatile.

Pots of winter pansies will flower from autumn right through winter and produce a second burst of flowers in March. They thrive in the warmth of big cities and in the south of Britain. Farther north they benefit from being close to a house wall radiating heat.

Pansies are part of the viola family, which includes pansies, violas, violets and violettas. Pansies have a sweet scent, so put the container where you can catch the fragrance. Violas are also fragrant, and many new varieties will also flower from mid February. Viola flowers are smaller and less flamboyant than those of a winter pansy, and there is not the same colour range, although some have blotches at the centre of the flower. However, they are tougher and more compact.

A different display

One of the best ways to display winter pansies is in a theatre, like the one on the right, traditionally used to house collections of auricula flowers. The theatre not only gives the plants protection from winter weather, it also allows you to make a big display with relatively few plants. The low stature of winter pansies also makes them a pretty foil for larger foliage plants, such as grasses and heathers.

Growing pansies

Although they will endure some shade, for best results stand pots where they will catch all the available sun that winter days can offer. Use a good multipurpose compost with a generous layer of drainage to allow heavy

A sunny posy of golden pansies encircle a flowering heather that has been dyed yellow (left). The wicker basket on a low twiggy table keeps them safe from frost and easy to view.

Echo the colour of your pansies in their pot so it does not dominate the display. Twirls of *Carex rubra* (right) tone with crimson winter pansies in a warm terracotta jar.

A wooden 'auricula theatre' (centre) houses a winter pansies and violas. Rearrange the display when you feel like a new look, moving pots, or adding fresh plants or souvenirs from a winter walk.

Simple pansies get formal when paired (far right) with the glossy black grass, *Ophiopogon planiscapus* 'Nigrescens' in a sharp-edged galvanised box.

winter rain to run through quickly before it can chill the roots, and add a handful of Perlite to soak up excess moisture. As a final aid to drainage, raise the pot on feet or place a few pieces of broken pot or stones underneath it.

Try to buy more pansies than you need and keep the surplus to one side, ready to replace any that fail. Discard pansies at the end of their flowering season – you will get better results with fresh plants the following year. Use fresh compost for your summer pansy display, or you might encourage an outbreak of debilitating 'pansy sickness'.

Key facts

- **Hardy and vigorous**, winter pansies (*Viola x wittrockiana*) are large-flowered hybrid pansies, which provide rich, deep colour for winter containers. There are a number of colour series, but most have markings or 'faces' at the centre of each flower and some have a thin rim of a different colour at the outer edge of the petals.
- **Bingo, Delta, Fama and Imperial Series** all have large blooms in a range of colours, with and without central blotches.
- **The Universal Series** is an intermediate size with a broad range of single colours, often with a central blotch.
- **The Ultima Series**, such as 'Regal' and 'Joker', have medium-sized flowers in a range of attractive colours.

When it is too cold to venture into the garden, turn your attention to the house and plant festive container arrangements to decorate a conservatory or to give visitors a cheery welcome.

Rich, deep colours are a favourite choice for decorating at Christmas. Scarlet poinsettias, *Euphorbia pulcherrima*, are as much a part of the festive season as the Norway spruce. But the apricot and cream tones of the marble poinsettia used in the planting on page 77, and the soft pink of the smaller pot, bring a new twist to the tradition. These subtle shades set the tone for a soft-coloured indoor display for a bright window or conservatory.

Feature plant

At the centre of the display stands an *Amaryllis* 'Apple Blossom' flanked by two coppery square pots of *Phalaenopsis*

Add a touch of festive paint

A metallic varnish was rubbed onto the square terracotta pots featured here, to give a warm copper glow that enhances the pink tones of the blooms. A scattering of shimmering wooden apples and hazelnuts completes the display.

Silvered rims pick up the glint of the fine tinsel draped through the branches of these matching spruces. The trees will sparkle on frosty mornings, but the warm terracotta of the pots ensures that the overall feel is not too cold.

orchids. Each amaryllis bulb produces one or two thick stems with huge, sweet-smelling blooms, but the flowerheads can be rather top heavy and may appreciate the support of metal flower markers or long twigs, which look more attractive than the usual bamboo canes.

Phalaenopsis orchids, which are also known as moth orchids, are perfect for this collection as they tolerate shade and are quite happy with good indirect light, which also suits the amaryllis and poinsettia. Their heads nod on slender stems and fill the centre of the container.

Seasons greetings

Bringing seasonal cheer to your home does not have to be restricted to the indoors. In the alternative grouping on the left, two blue spruce Christmas trees stand on stone steps leading up to a front door. Their thick foliage provides an aromatic invitation, drawing guests into the house.

Thick bows of dyed garden raffia add a further festive touch to the green and silver colour scheme, and break the hard lines of the tapered pots.

Tall stems of amaryllis bring height and grace to this arrangement, with the pale pinky white trumpet-shaped flowerheads drawing the eye to the top of the collection.

If you can have only a few containers, plan to keep them blooming with a succession of flowers that will take you through from the chills of winter to the bright days of spring.

Continuous planting is an effective way of making an impact with spring bulbs. They often look most dramatic when a single variety is planted densely in the container to create a block of colour. Plant in autumn, choosing plants so that as one pot of flowers starts to fade, the next will be ready to bloom.

The starting point for this display (far right) was a large-bloomed crocus: *Crocus vernus* 'Blue'. This was followed by the early flowering trumpet daffodil, *Narcissus* 'Rijnveld's Early Sensation' (below left). It grows to only 30cm and stands up well in winter winds. The third planting is soft pink 'Angélique' tulips (below right), chosen because it is one of the last tulips to flower.

Prepare ahead for success

Plant crocus bulbs in your container in September. All bulbs need the largest pot you can manage for maximum protection against frost. Even hardy bulbs can suffer in a small pot because they get frost from all directions – top, bottom and sideways.

The best compost for bulbs is John Innes No.1, with an added handful each of multipurpose compost and grit. Plant bulbs no more than an inch apart or even touching; avoid gaps in a container display. Plant the daffodils at the same time as the crocus in another pot, or in several if that is more convenient. It doesn't matter if these pots look a little shabby, because the flowers will be moved into your chosen pot for the display. You can plant the tulip bulbs as late as November, again in spare containers.

Put all the pots in a sheltered place to grow, ready to be brought forward one at a time. Deadhead after flowering, then lift the plants to make room for the next ones. The old bulbs can be moved into your borders, or into other pots to die off and be stored until next year.

The wineglass-shaped flowers of *Crocus vernus* (right) open wide in even the weakest rays of winter sun to reveal bright orange stamens. Packed tightly in a pot, they make a vibrant pool of colour.

A frilly collar of winter aconites sets off the robust blooms of the daffodil, 'Rijnveld's Early Sensation' and softens the lines of the square pot (far left). The golden display makes a bright contrast to the earlier purple crocuses.

Last in the pot are the 'Angélique' tulips (left). The buds will not open until early May, so there is no danger of them needing to go into the container while the daffodils are still looking splendid.

Plant winter flowers for an early start

You can experiment with other bulbs in succession. Winter aconites and muscari are good early choices, followed by hyacinths, or different varieties of daffodils and tulips.

- **For an earlier start** than the crocus, combine snowdrops and *Iris reticulata*. The variety 'George' (right) has velvety purple petals and is well-suited to growing in pots.

- **Buy snowdrops that are already sprouting**, or 'in the green'. *Galanthus caucasicus* and *G. elwesii* will flower the first year they are planted, but most varieties, including the common snowdrop, *G. nivalis* will not.

Pot practicalities

Successful container gardening depends to a large extent on the planning and work put in at the beginning. There's more to a great display than just putting a plant in a pot and hoping for the best.

Think about the pot and plants you want for your display at the same time, bearing in mind where you plan to put it and what else is growing nearby. If you are shopping for the pot and plants together it can be helpful to choose the pot first and then wheel it round with you as you select the plants.

Selecting the right pot

It is essential to choose a pot that is the right size for the plant or plants you intend to put in it. A container that is too small will soon become full of roots; it will be difficult to feed and water adequately and the plants will suffer. Conversely, a young plant in an over-large pot can also struggle, because the compost will remain wet for long periods.

If you want to keep the plant for several years – for example, a camellia or a shrub that will grow large when mature – and are starting with a young specimen, it is better to pot it on when necessary into a series of successively larger containers, than to start it off in an over-large tub.

Choosing your plants wisely

Do not select the tallest or largest specimen, or the one with the most open flowers when you are buying plants. Instead, opt for one that is bushy and bursting with health. Whether you are planting a large tree or a tiny alpine, follow the same basic rules for choosing your plant well.

First look under the pot. An established plant will fill its pot with roots and some may be visible through the drainage holes. If a plant resists when you lift it, it may have rooted into the bed it is standing on. This indicates that the plant has been in the same

Each time you repot, increase the diameter of the container by about 10cm.

Check under the pot. A well-established plant should show some roots growing out of the holes in its pot.

pot (and untouched in the garden centre) for some time and is quite likely to be pot-bound. Pulling the roots out of the bed will damage them, and you will almost certainly find it difficult to remove the pot for planting when you get home.

A straggly habit, obvious signs of pests or disease, poor leaf colour and dry compost, and moss and weeds on the top of the pot are all indications of neglect. You should also avoid newly potted plants which have been put on sale before they have had a chance to re-establish themselves. If the compost looks fluffy and new, or if the plant seems loose when tugged gently, you may have difficulty replanting it without damaging the roots.

Getting your plant settled

When you get a new plant home, give it a good soaking even if the compost appears moist. If it is at all dry, it is best to water and then wait a day before planting to allow it to recover. After planting, water your arrangement in well, then wait until the compost is starting to dry out before watering it again.

HOW TO PICK A HEALTHY PLANT

It is clear which of the two *Ajuga reptans* below ① is healthy, and which is suffering from neglect. But two simple checks will eliminate less obvious problem plants.

- Check under the pot ② for weeds and signs of infestation, such as the slug here.
- Lift the leaves and look for evidence of damage and disease. The sick plant ③ is thin and its leaves have been nibbled, while the healthier plant ④ bursts with new growth.

If a pot is hard to lift from the bed it is standing on, it may have been in its pot for too long and may be damaged by being moved (near right, top).

Pull the plant gently (near right, below). If it is loose, it may be lightly rooted and difficult to replant.

A thick covering of moss and weeds on the top of a container plant (centre) are a sign that it has been neglected.

Check the compost (far right). If it is too new, the plant may not survive being repotted.

Drainage and compost

Choosing the right compost is crucial to the eventual success of a container display, especially if you are growing plants that won't grow in your garden soil. Different plants also have very different moisture requirements, so ensure that you do not over or under water them.

Good drainage is essential to prevent waterlogging, which will eventually kill plants, so make sure every pot has plenty of holes in the base.

Letting the water drain away freely

Water will escape more freely through several small evenly spaced holes than one large hole. Your pot will also need a good layer of drainage material in the base to prevent the holes from getting blocked.

Coarse gravel, or broken crocks are the traditional choice for drainage but many other substances including crumbled polystyrene are suitable as well. Whatever you use, fill the container to a tenth of its total height.

However well water drains through the compost, it will not be able to run free if the pot is standing on the ground. Raise the pot by standing it on bricks or similar flat objects, taking care not to cover up the drainage holes. Or add a professional finishing touch with ornamental pot feet.

Other drainage options

If you prefer to stand your containers in saucers, you will need to keep a careful eye on them. The saucers will retain surplus water, which can cause the roots to freeze in winter. The benefit of saucers is that you can leave plants standing in a little water when going away for a few days to make sure that they have enough moisture. Saucers also prevent freshly watered pots on balconies dripping onto neighbours living below.

Some plants, particularly herbs, succulents, alpines and Mediterranean species require perfect drainage. Grey-leaved plants, such as *Artemesia* 'Powis Castle', *Brachyglottis* 'Sunshine' and *Perovskia* 'Blue Spire' are good examples.

Make more holes with a drill (near right, top) if necessary, using a masonry bit at a slow speed for terracotta.

You may need to punch out holes where marked on plastic pots (near right, bottom).

A number of small holes are more effective for providing drainage than a single larger hole (centre right, top)

Crumbled polystyrene plant trays are a lightweight and inexpensive drainage option (far right top).

Succulent plants (far right) need perfect drainage to thrive in containers.

Choosing the best growing medium

There are two basic kinds of compost: those containing soil and those that are soil free and are based on peat. If you are concerned about the environmental effects of cutting peat, choose a soil-free compost made with a peat substitute. These are usually based on coir, and may need extra fertilisers and more frequent watering.

Soil-free composts

Proprietory 'container' or 'multipurpose' composts are generally soil-free with a slow-release feed, wetting agent and sometimes with water-retaining gel added.

All soil-free composts contain additives, such as lime to reduce their acidity, sharp sand to improve drainage, and a fast-acting fertiliser. They are excellent for a summer display, but tend to tire quickly, so are less suitable for permanent plantings. Lighter than soil-based composts, they are a good choice for balconies and roof gardens where the weight of the pots needs to be carefully considered.

Soil-based composts

Composts containing soil are a mixture of loam, peat and sharp sand, and are largely based on the 'John Innes' formula. They contain varying amounts of fertiliser, depending on what they are to be used for.

John Innes No.1 contains very little fertiliser, making it suitable for young plants, which do not grow well in high levels of plant food. John Innes No.2 has twice as much fertiliser as No.1. It can be used for fast-growing young plants and for slow-growing plants which will be over-stimulated by too much fertiliser.

For large or mature specimens use John Innes No.3. This contains three times as much plant food as No.1 and will be able to sustain plants in the same container for a number of years.

If you want to grow thriving acid-loving plants, such as rhododendrons, you will need an acid compost. These composts are lime free and are usually labelled 'ericaceous'. They also have plant foods added as well.

If you are growing herbs, alpines, succulents and Mediterranean species, you can improve the drainage of proprietary composts by adding fine grit (top left) or sharp sand (centre left). You will usually need about 10 per cent by volume. If it is important to minimise the weight – for example, if your pots are on a balcony – add perlite (bottom left) or horticultural vermiculite instead.

Water the compost before you begin to add your plants. When planting is complete, water again and add a layer of mulch on top to lock in the moisture.

Mulching brings many benefits over and above its primary role in improving the soil. It gives your pots a net, well-tended appearance and reduces the amount of time and effort you need to spend on routine care.

Extreme weather is not kind to bare soil. Hot sunshine and winds dry and harden the surface, which causes the soil to crack. Pounding rain can turn the surface to a caked crust and wash away plant food and even the soil surface.

Why use a mulch?

Some container plantings are so dense that the surface of the compost is hidden. However, if the compost is exposed, it is vulnerable to invasion by weeds, and moisture will evaporate from it in hot weather, making frequent watering essential. The answer is to cover the compost with a layer of mulch (see the examples below), which will help to reduce these problems.

Other benefits of mulching

As well as protecting your soil and suppressing weeds, mulching can also improve soil texture, provide the plants with nutrients, deter certain pests and protect plant roots from extreme temperatures including moderate frost. Mulches can also add visual interest and texture to your pots.

Standard trees, if not underplanted, and fountain-like plants, such as agaves (right), leave a lot of exposed compost on the top of the pot. Make the most of the space by adding decorative and imaginative arrangements of differently coloured pebbles or mixed mulches.

A coloured mulch adds flair to a contemporary planting. Recycled glass chippings (right) twinkle in the light, while coloured gravel, such as ice white, or coal black have a more subtle effect. Match the colour of the flowers, pot or surroundings for a professional finishing touch.

Using mulches with containers

Bark chippings and cocoa shells sold for mulching garden borders are also suitable for containers. Heavy mulches, such as pebbles, have the extra benefit of adding weight to plastic pots, which might otherwise blow over. The extra weight can also help to deter doorstep thieves.

Use a mulch to add an original decorative touch of your own to a container display. Think about the container and the plants you are using and choose a mulch that will set them off to perfection. For example, stones and gravel can add a stylish twist to containers. Use a honey-coloured gravel with terracotta or white chippings to highlight a pot. Mix materials, such as slate and gravel for a natural 'scree' effect or pile on smoothly rounded pebbles.

Use natural mulches to give your pots a theme. A little moss from the garden, or a few pine cones or conkers gathered on a walk, all work well with woodland plants and shrubs. Shells, which can be bought in many shops and should never be picked up from the beach, will instantly evoke the sea – whether you are nearby or not.

Follow these simple guidelines and your containers should flourish from the day you plant them. By taking care early on, you will reap the benefits throughout the life of the display.

The first step when planting a container is to put a layer of drainage material in the base. This allows water to drain away but stops the compost slipping out of the pot. Fill the pot to a tenth of its height with crushed brick, coarse gravel, small stones, smashed terracotta or bits of broken polystyrene trays.

Adding compost

Once you have a good drainage layer, add compost until the container is about two-thirds full. Push down with your fingers to firm it very gently. Do not ram it down hard; air is needed for a healthy root system, and compressing the compost makes it hard for plants to root into.

Placing the plants

Begin to introduce the plants, starting with the largest. Do not dig a hole: instead, draw the compost back with a trowel, place your plant in the space created, then let the compost fall back around it.

Ease plants out of their pots or trays, and unless the label says otherwise, plant them at the depth they were in their original pots. Add compost as you go so that smaller specimens are at the right level. Leave at least 2.5cm between the surface of the compost and the rim of the pot.

Filling in

When your plants are in position, fill around the roots with compost, firming gently to get rid of any large air pockets. Then water well and top up the compost if it has settled. Now is the time to tuck a discreet plant label at the back of the pot.

Put the pot in position

Finally, position the pot. It is best to raise it off the ground on pot feet to prevent the drainage holes from becoming clogged.

Choose a compost that is suitable for your plants and fill the pot to about two-thirds of its depth (right)

Firm the compost very gently around the plant ensuring that you don't pack it too tightly around the roots (far right).

Put the largest plant in first (above) having pulled the compost gently back with a trowel. Carefully push your plants out (top left) and plant them to the same depth as the pot they have come out of.

Water newly planted pots (top right) thoroughly before setting them in their final position.

Planting a hanging basket

A globe of solid colour or a shaggy mass of blooms swinging by a door or window will brighten any outlook. Follow these simple steps for guaranteed success with hanging baskets and flower balls.

There are many different styles of wire hanging baskets and liners available. If the basket will be covered by plants a plain one will suffice. If the basket will show, choose a decorative one and line it with moss, if you have plenty around the edges of your lawn, or dyed coir, a moss substitute that will remain green for longer than the real thing.

Create a base

Add a layer of moss, then place an old saucer in the bottom to prevent water from running straight out through the moss, then add a layer of compost up to the height you want your first plants. If you are using a cardboard liner, cut out holes where you want the plants before you add the compost.

Introduce your first ring of plants pushing them between the wires from the inside of the basket out. Use young specimens for the sides: they will be easier to push through than mature plants and will establish quickly, hanging down to create a pretty trailing effect. Continue adding moss, compost and plants and work your way up the sides of the basket. Hanging baskets look best when packed with plants, so the demands on the compost are great. Include some water-retaining gel, or 'swelly gelly' and slow-release plant food now to make the maintenance of your basket easier throughout the season.

Finally plant the top with taller, more erect species in the middle and trailing ones around the edge to hide the rim.

Making a flower ball

You can make a flower ball by planting the sides and bases of two separate hanging baskets and joining them together. Follow the instructions below for planting a single, wire hanging basket to make the lower half of the ball. Position your first plants close to the bottom of the basket, to avoid having a bald patch on the underside. Leave the top of the basket unplanted, but make sure that it is filled with compost.

If your aim is to grow a mass of trailing plants you can use a plain basket and utilitarian liner (near right), because they will be hidden when the plants are mature.

Cover the basket base and about the first 5cm of the sides with a layer of moss or moss substitute (middle right).

Next plant a second basket to make the top of the ball. Remove the chains and put a small upturned plastic flower pot in the bottom. Working around the pot, plant the basket up as before. Finish off by firming down the compost. Water both baskets well, and if this causes the compost to settle, top it up so that it is level with the rim.

Place a thin sheet of wood or an old plate on top of the upper basket to support the compost. Turn the basket over and place it on top of the lower basket. Gently withdraw the wood or plate and secure the two baskets together with lengths of garden wire. Hang the flower ball by the chains of the lower basket, taking care not to squash the plants in the upper basket as you do so.

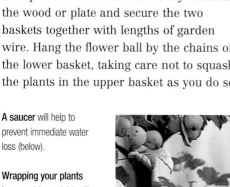

A saucer will help to prevent immediate water loss (below).

Wrapping your plants in paper (above right) will protect them as you work.

The finished basket should be thickly planted; the trailing plants will hide a less attractive container.

Watering

The most time-consuming aspect of growing in containers is watering. In summer you may need to water each pot twice a day, but follow this simple advice and you can make light work of the job.

Pots and other containers hold a comparatively small amount of compost, which dries out fast, particularly when plants are growing and taking up a lot of water. The compost in containers is also usually warmer than soil at ground level, which encourages drying out in hot weather. Fortunately, there are several simple ways to make watering easier and less time-consuming.

Water-retaining gels

The absorption properties of compost can be improved by adding water-retaining gels. The water-laden granules, or gel, gradually give off moisture into the surrounding compost as it dries out. And each time you water the container, the gel absorbs more water than the compost, thus retaining moisture in the pot for longer.

Mixing the gel

Many packet instructions advise you to rehydrate the crystals first, then mix the sticky wet gel into the compost. But this is a messy job and it can be difficult making sure that the 'swelly gelly' is evenly distributed. It is easier to mix dry granules into the compost and then add the water, but remember that the mixture will swell once it is watered, so you can easily over-fill the container. Err on the side of caution, then top up the pot with more compost if it seems to be necessary.

Self-watering pots

Self-watering containers can reduce the need to water pots daily, but are still only as good as the person looking after them. It is easy for plants to become over-wet in rainy weather or, conversely, be forgotten and allowed to dry out. However, they can be very useful if you know you don't have time for watering every day. Some systems have a false base which acts as a reservoir for water. More sophisticated containers also have a tube for refilling and overflow holes to allow excess water to drain away.

Give pots a soaking in the morning (right), before the sun gets too harsh, or early in the evening. At midday the water may evaporate before it can reach the roots or may even cause the leaves to scorch.

Water-retaining gels or 'swelly gelly' (far left), look like sugar crystals when dry, but are capable of absorbing many times their own volume of water, and when fully wet they resemble cooked tapioca.

A self-watering hanging basket, pot or trough (near left) works because it has a false bottom, beneath which is a reservoir to hold water. The compost is kept moist by drawing water up into the pot when it is needed through a matting pad and wick.

Maintenance

A little extra attention will extend the life of arrangements that are intended to last for one season only, and is essential if you are to keep permanent plantings looking their best for many years. With food, drink and a snug container, your displays will flourish from season to season.

All plants need a regular source of food if they are to reach their full potential. Always follow the manufacturer's recommendations – overdosing can be toxic, while underfeeding will not allow plants to reach their full potential.

Types of fertiliser

Liquid and soluble powder fertilisers are fast acting and quickly absorbed by plants, but must be applied regularly because their effects are short-lived. Use them during the growing season and reduce the application gradually once the plants have passed their peak. You don't need to feed plants in winter even if they still look good, because they are not in active growth.

Foliar feeds are liquid fertilisers in a highly diluted form capable of being absorbed through a plant's leaves; these are useful to boost performance for a special occasion, or as a pick-me-up.

Fertilisers also come in powder and capsule forms. They can be fast acting or release their nutrients gradually over a period of up to 12 months, according to the outside temperature and the moisture of the compost.

Spraying

Using spraying as a preventive measure is no longer necessary, as most modern cultivars are more disease-resistant than traditional varieties. But if fungal diseases,

Slow-release fertilisers (left) are best for container gardening. Mix into your compost at planting time. Or use special hanging basket slow-release feeds in 'tea bag' form, included when you plant.

With permanently planted containers, push in fertiliser pellets (centre), or sprinkle on a top-dressing of granules (above) in spring. Dense displays, such as hanging baskets, may need additional liquid feeds when they are flowering.

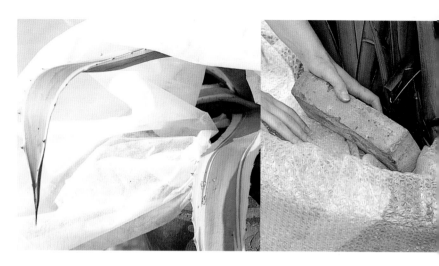

Cover the plant (near right) with a couple of layers of horticultural fleece, or, if this is not available, some old net curtain can be used instead.

In a prolonged cold spell, it is wise to employ some additional protection for your terracotta pots. The best way to do this is to envelope the pot using either bubble wrap, several layers of cardboard or a piece of old carpet.

such as blackspot, rust and scab, were a problem in permanent container displays one year, it may be wise to spray plants early in the following season before signs of similar damage appear.

An instant trigger spray of the right insecticide or general fungicide may be all you need. However, you may prefer to use a pressure sprayer if you have a large number of plants, in a conservatory, or if you have many awkward-to-reach hanging baskets.

Some chemicals are available as a puffer dust, but this looks unsightly where it accumulates around a pot.

Deadheading

Cutting off spent flowers tidies up the plants, removes dead material which can become infected, stops the plant putting unnecessary effort into seed production, and encourages new shoots to grow.

It is possible to deadhead many plants by snapping off the spent blooms with your fingernails, but sharp scissors or secateurs deal more cleanly with geraniums and patio roses. Always make your cut just above a leaf joint to prevent stems from dying-back.

Traditionally roses were deadheaded and pruned at the same time, by cutting back to a bud somewhere down the new season's stem. More recent tests suggest that you will have healthier bushes if you leave on as

much foliage as possible throughout summer, and just cut off any dead flowerheads.

Keeping plants warm in winter

Many patio plants are not fully hardy and may be badly frosted or killed in very cold weather. Insulating the container helps to keep the roots warm, but the foliage can also be protected. Keep frost at bay by wrapping layers of newspaper lightly around the foliage, but remove it when the temperature rises to give plants access to light. Never use polythene: it will stop the plant from breathing and will cause sweating that can lead to grey mould, or botrytis and rotting.

With a little care many traditional 'basket plants', will survive to flower again. *Begonia semperflorens*, fuchsias, bedding geraniums and trailing petunias are all really tender perennials and can be over-wintered in a light place with a minimum temperature of 5°C (40°F).

Most hardy plants need no special winter protection, as long as they are in containers that are substantial enough to insulate the roots in very cold weather. However, it is drought, not frozen roots, that will kill a plant at this time – when the pot freezes, plants are unable to extract moisture from the compost.

Surprisingly few pests affect container-grown plants – far fewer than in the open garden. You may notice the odd bite out of a leaf or petal, but these isolated incidents seldom merit the wholesale use of chemical controls. Only one or two stubborn pests need chemicals to effectively get rid of them.

As a rule, the fewer chemicals you splash around, the more beneficial insects – particularly lacewings and ladybirds, but even wasps and hoverflies – will move in and do the job for you. These mini-predators have voracious appetites for aphids and other insect pests, and with care it is possible to establish a good balance between friend and foe.

You can even buy beneficial insect larvae to introduce into the garden, but if you do this, you will need to avoid chemical controls completely – you don't want to kill off your 'good insects'. Also, unless you retain a number of insect pests as a food source, your population of 'goodies' will eventually die out.

If you prefer not to use pesticides to get rid of aphids (above), a solution of soft soap in a spray bottle is an effective organic alternative.

Though snails (left) and slugs are deterred by hard surfaces, they still gravitate towards certain plants. Deterrence is often a more effective way of dealing with them than all-out attack.

Slugs and snails

Although slugs and snails will attack plants grown in pots, they will not cause as many problems as in the open garden, as they dislike hard surfaces. Putting a gravel mulch on top of a pot, may act as a deterrent, but the best control is to inspect containers regularly and remove any slugs and snails you find. Slug pellets often seem to attract more than they destroy, but a liquid slug control watered over the container will help to deal with severe cases of infestation.

Aphids

The most common pests on container plants are aphids. Although usually referred to as 'greenfly', aphids come in many colours and sizes. They are small sap-sucking insects, and disfigure plants, usually on young shoots, but occasionally elsewhere. The pansy aphid, for example, colonises the stems just above soil level. Damage caused by aphids tends to be more unsightly than fatal. However, in the case of pansy, lettuce and carrot-willow aphids (which can devastate parsley and other herbs of the same family), you may become aware of the problem only when the plants start to lose condition, by which time it is often too late to do anything about it.

Aphids can be controlled by a number of insecticides. One, pirimicarb, is specific to the pest and will not harm natural predators such as ladybirds. Aphids can also spread viruses among plants and indirectly cause the fungal disease sooty mould. The fungus lives on the sticky honeydew the aphids secrete and, if left unattended, clogs up plant pores. The best way to deal with this is to wash the affected plant with a weak solution of warm water and washing-up liquid.

Vine weevils

The most serious pest to container gardeners is the grub of the vine weevil. The adult, a black, flightless insect is not harmful to plants. But its dirty white larvae, which hatch in compost, feed off the roots of plants. By the time a plant begins to wilt, it will be too late to save it.

Avoiding boggy conditions will help, or you could try applying a long-lasting, systemic insecticide, imidacloprid (or Provado) to plant roots as a drench. Even if you haven't had vine weevils this is a good preventive measure, and also controls a wide range of other pot plant pests.

Animal pests

Larger nuisances can also be a problem in the garden. A cat will be sure to curl up in the middle of your choicest container with no heed for the unfortunate plant, and dogs will often pee against pots or dig up newly planted bulbs or seedlings.

The best way to deter cats is to insert lots of short canes, which will be hidden as the plants grow. To save leaves from the burning effects of dog urine, place a pot in a large outer pot or raise it off the ground. You can also train dogs not to use a particular part of the garden.

Squirrels have a nose for bulbs, and can often be caught digging in pots. Putting a layer of chicken wire on the top of the compost may put them off.

Vine weevil grubs (top) have become more common with the use of soil-free composts, and thrive in waterlogged containers.

Making life uncomfortable for cats is probably the best way to keep them away from your pots.

Hungry squirrels (right) can play havoc with freshly planted bulbs. A strong-smelling product called Renardine may help to deter them.

Massed together, and warmed by heat reflected from paving and walls,
plants in pots offer an ideal environment for viruses and fungi to spread,
but with care and hygiene, you can keep your container plants disease-free.

Prevention of disease begins at potting
time, when you must make sure that all
your containers are scrupulously clean.
New pots should not need any cleaning, but
used pots should be washed. Wooden
containers will need to be vigorously
scrubbed, and treated periodically with
a timber preservative that will not harm
plants: rotting wood can harbour all kinds
of disease spores and undesirable bacteria.

This advice also applies to seed trays,
small plant pots and any containers used to
raise seedlings. Ideally, containers should be
washed as soon as they are emptied so that
they are ready for use when needed. Even
accessories such as canes and labels can
carry disease and should also be disinfected
before they are put into storage.

Cleaning any walls and paving slabs
around your pots regularly will remove the
dirt and algae that invariably collects. But
this does more than just make the patio look
better; it will also help to destroy any
disease-carrying organisms that may be
lurking in cracks and crevices.

Tool cleanliness is also crucial: many
diseases are passed from plant to plant
on dirty secateurs. When pruning, think of
yourself as a surgeon, and wipe the blades
of your secateurs thoroughly with a cloth
soaked in disinfectant before moving on
to the next plant.

Bacteria and fungi can also be spread
on your fingers, so remember to wash your
hands from time to time while working in
the garden.

Never reuse old compost. Not only will it
contain an imbalance of plant foods by the
end of the season, but it may also harbour
disease spores and bacteria, which will be
carried over to the next planting.

You can usually spread old compost over
the garden or on the compost heap.
However, certain diseases, such as tomato
and potato blight, contaminate the soil so
much that it is best to throw away any
compost that plants affected with these
problems have grown in.

Nip disease in the bud

Always remove dead flowers and leaves, and
any other unhealthy plant material as soon
as you spot them. Sweep the area around
your pots regularly, and never compost
anything that you know to be infected.

Like people, plants under stress are more
vulnerable to disease than those bursting
with vitality. Keep plants well fed to give
them the best chance of survival. Fertilisers

that are high in phosphates and potash produce strong root systems and tough, disease-resistant growth, while those with high levels of nitrogen can encourage lax, soft growth, which is easily invaded by diseases.

Underwatering also puts plants under stress, making them vulnerable to disease, while plants grown in waterlogged containers will have poor root health and weak, sickly growth.

Spotting the signs of disease

However careful you are, it is almost impossible to keep plants completely disease-free. Botrytis, powdery mildew, leaf spots and rust are common problems.

Spotty leaves that fall early are probably infected with leaf spot. If you discover an infection, remove affected leaves and spray with a fungicide to stop it from spreading.

Rust is very difficult to eliminate; only one or two of the fungicides available to the amateur gardener have any effect, so you will need to ask for advice or read all the labels on treatments before buying.

A velvety grey mould on leaves, flowers or fruit is caused by botrytis. Ideally clear away all dead parts of the plant and do not allow water to stand on leaves and soft shoots for long periods in dull weather. Remove affected plants before the problem spreads.

A dusty white coating on leaves is likely to be caused by powdery mildew. This is most common in warm dry weather and weakens the plant.

Curing the problem

One of the most effective and wide-ranging fungicides is sulphur, which is also approved for organic use. Some plants, particularly some varieties of gooseberry, are intolerant to it, so check before you spray.

If a particular plant is repeatedly affected, replace it with something more robust. And note that the best way to avoid problems is to choose disease-resistant varieties.

Disease is common on roses (left), which are very susceptible to black spot, powdery mildew and rust (right). A regular spray of fungicide will help to keep your container displays in peak condition.

Examples of leaf spot (below top), rust (below centre) and powdery mildew (bottom). All are caused by fungi and will spread particularly fast in overcrowded conditions.

100 Container plant directory

To help you to select the best plants for your containers, here are more than 200 chosen by experts and listed by colour and season. A cup symbol a indicates plants that have won the Royal Horticultural Society's Award of Garden Merit (AGM).

White & cream flowers

Spring

Anemone blanda
'White Splendour' ♀
Clump-forming perennial with irregularly lobed leaves and yellow-eyed, daisy-like flowers. This is a vigorous and free-flowering cultivar.
height & spread: 15x15cm
cultivation: In autumn, soak tubers overnight and plant 5cm deep. Place in full sun. Keep damp, but stop watering once foliage dies back. Keep tubers dry in pots or store in dry sand until replanting in autumn. You can produce more plants by careful division of tubers.

Crocus chrysanthus
'Cream Beauty' ♀
Early spring-flowering corm with rounded buttery cream flowers. The grass-like leaves have a central silver stripe.
height: 7.5cm
C. chrysanthus 'Ladykiller' ♀
Slender flowers with fine purple vein-like markings on outer petals and a yellow eye.
C. chrysanthus 'Snow Bunting' ♀ Rounded flowers, with grey-blue feathering

on the outer petals.
cultivation: Plant in autumn in John Innes No.1 with extra grit. Place corms at a depth of 8cm. Site in sun or light shade. Keep the compost moist but avoid waterlogging. Remove cormlets during dormancy to increase. Mice and voles eat crocus corms, especially newly planted ones. Birds may damage the flowers.

Lamium maculatum
Dead nettle
'White Nancy' ♀
Herbaceous perennial has creeping habit. Heart-shaped silver leaves with green margin. Hooded flowers are borne in dense spikes.
height & spread: 15x40cm
cultivation: Grow in shade in a humus-rich compost. Keep moist in spring and summer but drier in winter. Apply a balanced liquid feed monthly in the growing season.

Magnolia stellata
Star magnolia
'Waterlily' ♀
Spreading deciduous shrub, with star-shaped flowers, which emerge from pointed silky buds.
height & spread: Limited, in a pot, to about 1.8x1.8m
M. denudata ♀ Yulan/lily tree Goblet-shaped, lemon-scented flowers.
cultivation: Plant in early

autumn in John Innes No.3 with added leaf-mould. Site in sun or partial shade, sheltered from cold winds and frosts. Keep compost moist.
   Apply a weak liquid feed every month in growing season, and mulch with leaf-mould in autumn. Prune any frost-damaged branches in spring. Buy from a reputable nursery.

Pieris japonica
'Grayswood' ♀
Compact, bushy evergreen shrub with glossy dark green leaves, coppery when young. Creamy white flowers in clusters.
height & spread: 1.8x1.8m
P. japonica 'Debutante' ♀
Low-growing, to about 90cm with flowers carried in dense, erect clusters.
cultivation: Plant in autumn in acid compost, in dappled shade. Although hardy, frost will damage flower buds, so try to provide some shelter.
   Keep compost moist. Apply a liquid feed monthly in the growing season, and mulch in autumn with leaf-mould. Prune dead wood, and for shape, after the shrub has finished flowering.

Tulipa
Tulip
'Purissima'
Bulb producing large, cup-shaped, cream flowers and

grey-green leaves.
height: 20cm
T. 'Spring Green' ♀ Large, cup-shaped ivory flowers with feathery green markings.
height: 40cm
T. turkestanica ♀ Species tulip bearing up to ten blooms, star-shaped with yellow eyes.
T. 'White Triumphator' ♀ Lily-flowered tulip with pointed, reflexed petals.
cultivation: Plant bulbs in autumn, 10cm deep in a loam-based compost. Site pot in a sunny sheltered spot. Deadhead, and keep moist in growing season. Increase by removing daughter bulbs and growing them on.

Summer

Agapanthus africanus
African lily
'Albus' ♀
Evergreen perennial with arching, strap-like leaves. Trumpet-shaped flowers are held in rounded flowerheads on long stalks.
height & spread: 90x50cm
A. 'Snowy Owl' Hardy, deciduous variety.
A. 'White Dwarf' Small, frost-tender, evergreen cultivar.
height & spread: 40x30cm
cultivation: Grow in large pots of John Innes No.3, in a sunny sheltered site. Move tender varieties under glass in autumn.

A. 'Snowy Owl' may be left outside if given a sheltered position and a dry mulch. Water freely in spring and summer but keep almost dry in winter. Give a balanced liquid feed from spring until the flower buds form. Increase by dividing clumps.

Ajuga reptans
Bugle
'Alba'

Low-growing, evergreen perennial spreading by creeping stems. Tubular flowers are carried in whorls on erect spikes.
height & spread: 15x25cm
cultivation: Grow in dappled shade in a humus-rich potting mix. Keep compost moist at all times, and feed monthly in growth with a balanced liquid feed. Create new plants by removing and repotting the plantlets that form at the end of the creeping stems.

Argyranthemum foeniculaceum
Marguerite
'Royal Haze' ♀

Vigorous, evergreen sub-shrub with finely dissected, grey-green foliage. Mass of daisy-like flowers borne over a long season.
height & spread: 70x70cm
A. gracile 'Chelsea Girl' ♀ Has very finely cut, feathery foliage.
A. 'Snowflake' Has semi-double flowers.
cultivation: Plant in spring in a good-quality potting mix and site in full sun. Water freely throughout summer but keep compost almost dry in winter.

Feed fortnightly with a balanced liquid fertiliser. Encourage continued blooming by cutting off dead flowerheads.

Brugmansia
suaveolens ♀
Syn. *Datura suaveolens*
Angel's trumpet

Bears large, pendulous, trumpet-shaped flowers, which are highly scented, especially at night.
height & spread: 1.8x1.5m
B. suaveolens 'Variegata' Slightly smaller plant with cream-margined leaves.
cultivation: Grow in a large pot of John Innes No.3 in a greenhouse at a minimum 7°C. In summer, move outside to a sunny spot. Frost-damaged plants usually rejuvenate. Water freely in summer but keep almost dry in winter. Once established, feed fortnightly with a diluted liquid fertiliser. Deadhead often. Prune hard in spring. NB All parts of this plant are poisonous.

Cobaea scandens
f. alba ♀
Cup and saucer vine

Rapidly growing perennial vine, usually grown as an annual. Wide, cup-shaped flowers are white, ageing to cream. Cobaea climbs by means of tendrils.
height & spread: 2.4x1.5m
cultivation: Plant out young plants once frost has passed. Use a free-draining compost. Place pot in a sheltered sunny position. Provide support for the climbing stems, such as wires or trellis, on a wall. The compost should be

kept moist at all times, but avoid waterlogging. Feed throughout summer with a balanced liquid feed.

Convolvulus
cneorum ♀
Silverbush, shrubby bindweed

The leaves of this dwarf evergreen shrub are covered in silky hairs, giving the plant a silvery appearance. Pink-tinged buds open into white funnel-shaped flowers.
height & spread: 50x50cm
cultivation: Grow in pots of John Innes No.1 with added grit for extra drainage. Site in full sun. Water moderately while growing and sparingly in winter. Apply a weak liquid feed every month in the growing season.

Pruned back hard in spring if outgrowing its space. Prone to fungal and bacterial diseases in warm, wet conditions.

Dimorphotheca
pluvialis
Star of the veldt, Cape marigold
'Glistening White'

This compact, upright annual has deeply toothed, dark green leaves and bears a profusion of dark-eyed, daisy-like flowers.
height & spread: 30x23cm
D. sinuata 'Tetra Pole Star' Has large white flowers up to 7.5cm across.
cultivation: Plant out after the last frosts in pots of John Innes No.2 and place containers in a sunny site. The flowers tend to close up in dull weather. Although drought-tolerant,

growth is better when the plant is watered moderately. Apply a weak liquid feed every 2 weeks once flowering starts. Deadhead regularly to prolong flowering.

Felicia amelloides
'Read's White'

Evergreen sub-shrub, usually grown as an annual. Plants are compact and low-growing. Yellow-eyed, daisy-like flowers are carried on long stalks above the foliage from summer to early autumn.
height & spread: 30x40cm
F. amelloides 'White Variegated' Cream stippled variegation on the foliage.
cultivation: Plant out after frost has passed into good-quality potting mix and site the container in full sun.

Water freely and apply a balanced liquid feed every 2 weeks. Pinch out young plants to encourage bushiness. Cut off dead flower stalks to prolong flowering.

Hedychium spicatum
Ginger lily, garland flower

Tender, clump-forming perennial with large leaves and waxy spikes of exotic white flowers with orange bases and red stamens.
height & spread: 1.2mx60cm
H. coronarium Fragrant, butterfly-shaped flowers.
cultivation: Grow in pots of John Innes No.3 in a sunny, sheltered position. They are tender and can only be moved out of the greenhouse or conservatory in summer. Water freely and apply a

balanced liquid feed monthly while growing.

Move plants back under glass in autumn and keep compost almost dry in winter. Increase by dividing congested clumps in spring.

Iberis amara
Common candytuft
Vigorous, erect, branching annual with dense clusters of tiny, fragrant flowers.
height & spread: 30x15cm
I. amara 'Giant Hyacinth Flowered' Has particularly large flower spikes.
I. amara 'Pinnacle' Flowers are especially fragrant.
cultivation: Plant out in spring in a free-draining compost in full sun. Water freely, but avoid waterlogging, and apply a balanced liquid feed every 2 weeks. Prolong flowering by cutting back spent flower spikes.

Lilium
Lily
'Mont Blanc'
Produces waxy, creamy white, upward-facing, star-shaped, fragrant flowers with orange anthers.
height: 60cm
L. 'Casa Blanca'♀ Bears very large, scented flowers.
L. 'Sterling Star' Upward-facing flowers, with tiny brown spots inside petals.
cultivation: Plant bulbs in autumn at a depth of 3 times their own height. Use John Innes No.2, with a good layer of crocks in the bottom of the pot. Site in full sun with shelter. Water freely while growing and give a high potash feed once a month. Store

bulbs over winter in their pots, or lift them and store in boxes of damp sand in a cool dry place. Propagate by removing outer scales of bulbs and growing in trays of compost. Lily beetle may be troublesome.

Lobularia maritima
Sweet alyssum
Syn. *Alyssum maritimum*
'Snow Crystals'
Low-growing, compact annual. Tiny, 4-petalled flowers in dense, fragrant clusters are profuse throughout summer.
height & spread: 10x20cm
L. maritima 'Carpet of Snow' Compact, mound-forming, profuse white variety.
L. maritima 'Creamery' Bears abundant cream-coloured flowers.
cultivation: Grow plants in moderately fertile, free-draining compost in full sun. Water freely and feed every month with a liquid tomato feed. Clip over first flush of blooms to produce further flowers. Sow seed in pots outside in late spring or under glass in early spring.

Myrtus communis
Myrtle
Bushy evergreen shrub with glossy, dark green aromatic foliage, and fragrant flowers and purple-black berries in autumn.
height & spread: 1.2mx60cm
M. communis ssp. tarentina Shorter plant; with pink flowers and white berries.
M. communis 'Variegata' Has leaves edged in cream.

cultivation: Plant in autumn in large pots of John Innes No.3, and site in full sun. In cold areas move pot to a sheltered position over winter. Water freely while establishing – thereafter, myrtle is fairly drought-tolerant. Apply a balanced liquid feed monthly in the growing season.

Prune frost-damaged branches or to maintain the shape of the bush, in spring. Downy mildew may be a problem in damp conditions.

Nemophila maculata
Five spot
Compact, low-growing annual with bowl-shaped flowers. Petals have purple veins and deep violet blotch at tip. Spreading prostrate plant has pale green, deeply lobed foliage.
height & spread: 15x20cm
N. maculata 'Freckles' Petals are heavily dotted with tiny black speckles.
cultivation: Plant out after last frosts in a good-quality potting compost, and site in sun or partial shade.

Nemophila should be kept moist at all times. Feed monthly with a diluted tomato fertiliser.

Nierembergia caerulea
Cup flower
'Mont Blanc'
Low, spreading tender perennial, usually grown as an annual, with tiny dark green leaves and abundant yellow-eyed, bowl-shaped flowers from early summer until early autumn. It looks pretty around the rim of a pot.

height & spread: 20x20cm
cultivation: Plant out in pots of John Innes No.1 after the last frosts. Site containers in a warm sunny position.

Water moderately and apply a balanced liquid feed every month.

Osteospermum
'Silver Sparkler'♀
Evergreen sub-shrub bearing abundant purple-eyed, daisy-like flowers. Leaves have cream edges.
height & spread: 45x30cm
O. 'Weetwood'♀ One of the hardiest cultivars, its white petals are flushed purple underneath, and the flowers have a yellow eye.
O. 'Whirlygig'♀ Spoon-shaped petals flushed blue on reverse; grey-blue eye.
cultivation: Grow in John Innes No.2 and site in full sun. Drought-tolerant but perform better if watered moderately in summer. Increase hardiness by keeping quite dry in winter.

Feed monthly in growing season with a balanced liquid fertiliser. Deadhead to prolong flowering.

Sutera
Syn. Bacopa
'Snowflake'
Tiny heart-shaped leaves clothe trailing, spreading stems. Masses of small five-petalled flowers borne throughout summer. Makes an excellent trailing hanging basket plant.
height & spread: 40x30cm
cultivation: Plant out after frost has passed in a moderately fertile, free-draining compost. Sutera

thrives in a sunny site or in partial shade.

Water freely but don't waterlog. Apply liquid tomato feed every 2 weeks.

Trim back after flowering and move plants to a heated greenhouse or conservatory over winter.

Tagetes erecta
African marigold
'Vanilla'
Large, cream-coloured pompom flowers are held over deeply cut, dark green foliage. Vigorous and free-flowering, it is the palest of all marigolds.
height & spread: 35x20cm
cultivation: Plant out in early summer after frost has passed, in pots of John Innes No.2. Flowers best in full sun.

Water freely in dry weather and apply a liquid tomato fertiliser every 2 weeks – overfeeding will encourage foliage at the expense of flowers. Deadhead regularly. They are prone to botrytis (grey mould) and loved by slugs.

Autumn

Abelia chinensis
Syn. Abelia rupestris
Small deciduous shrub with fragrant, funnel-shaped flowers, flushed pink on the outside. Flowers are carried in rounded clusters.
height & spread: 80x80cm
cultivation: Plant in spring or autumn in pots of John Innes No.3, and site in full sun. *Abelia chinensis* benefits from the shelter of a south-facing wall. Water freely in summer

but avoid waterlogging. Apply a balanced liquid feed monthly in spring and summer. Prune for shape directly after flowering.

Calluna vulgaris
Heather, Scots heather, ling
'White Lawn'
Dwarf, hardy evergreen shrub with trailing habit that is ideal for troughs. 'White Lawn' is just 5cm in height. It has white flowers amid clear green leaves.
height & spread: 5x30cm
C. vulgaris 'Kinlochruel'♀ Double-flowered cultivar. The foliage colour turns bronze in winter.
C. vulgaris 'Spring Cream'♀ Dark green foliage with cream tips in spring. Single white flowers.
height & spread: 25x30cm
cultivation: Plant in autumn into ericaceous (acid) compost and site pots in full sun. Do not allow the compost to dry out. Feed monthly in the growing season with a balanced liquid fertiliser.

Clip back flower spikes once they are past their best. Botrytis (grey mould) occur in humid conditions.

Crinum x powellii
'Album'♀
Bulbous, deciduous perennial with long, arching strap-shaped leaves. Large, trumpet-shaped flowers are borne in umbels (rounded flowerheads) at the top of sturdy flower stalks.
height & spread: 90x60cm
cultivation: Plant in spring with the neck of the bulb just above soil level. Use

John Innes No.2 with added sharp sand. Site in a sheltered, sunny spot. Water freely while in growth, applying a diluted tomato fertiliser monthly. Remove spent flowers. Increase by lifting and dividing congested clumps of bulbs in spring. Repot only when necessary.

Winter

Erica x darleyensis
Heath, heather
'White Perfection'♀
Compact, bushy evergreen shrub with small, bright green needle-like leaves and bell-shaped flowers in clusters at tips of shoots.
height & spread: 40x40cm
E. x *darleyensis* 'Springwood White'♀ Very low-growing.
E. x *darleyensis* 'White Glow' Compact at only 25cm tall.
height & spread: 15x40cm
cultivation: Plant in autumn in humus-rich compost. Site in full sun.

Water freely and apply a weak liquid fertiliser every month. Clip dead flower spikes back to encourage a second flush. Botrytis (grey mould) may develop in warm, wet conditions.

Galanthus nivalis
Snowdrop
Bulb producing dainty, hanging flowers with 3 outer petals partially concealing 3 green-marked inner petals.
height: 10cm
G. nivalis 'Flore Pleno'♀ Vigorous, double-flowered.
G. nivalis 'Pusey Green Tip' Broad double flowers with green markings on both inner and outer petals.

cultivation: In autumn plant bulbs 10cm deep in loam-based compost with extra leaf-mould. Site in sun or shade. Keep moist after planting. Increase by division after flowering.

Sarcococca hookeriana
var. digyna
Christmas box
Compact evergreen shrub with glossy dark green, lance-shaped leaves. Small, highly scented flowers are borne in tassel-like clusters in the leaf axils. Flowers are followed by shiny, purple-black berries.
height & spread: 75x75cm
cultivation: Plant in autumn in pots of John Innes No.3 and site in deep or partial shade. Sarcococca is drought-tolerant once established, but grows better with moderate watering. Feed once a month from spring to autumn, using a balanced liquid fertiliser.

Prune to improve shape in spring. You can produce more plants by cutting off and transplanting rooted suckers in autumn.

Viburnum tinus
Bushy evergreen shrub with glossy dark green foliage. Flowers are carried in large flat heads and are pink or red when in bud.
height & spread: 1.8x1.8m
V. tinus 'Lucidum' Very large flowerheads.
cultivation: Plant in autumn in pots of John Innes No.3, and site in sun or partial shade. Keep compost moist and feed shrub every month during the growing

season, using a balanced liquid fertiliser.

Trim shrub to shape after flowering. May be affected by aphids and sooty mould.

Pink flowers

Spring

Bellis perennis
Bedding daisy
'Dresden China' ♀
Double pompom flowers are carried on short stems above rosettes of green leaves.
height & spread: 15x10cm
B. perennis 'Galaxy Rose' Semi-double flowers with a yellow eye.
B. perennis 'Tasso Deep Rose' Flat-topped pompoms.
cultivation: Plant in autumn in free-draining, humus-rich compost. Site pot in sun or partial shade. Water moderately and apply a balanced liquid feed once the buds have formed.

Deadhead regularly to prolong flowering.

Camellia x williamsii
'Donation' ♀
Broad, upright, evergreen shrub with glossy dark green foliage and masses of semi-double, rose-pink flowers with darker veins.
height & spread: 1.8x1.5m
C. x *williamsii* 'Bowen Bryant' ♀ Erect open habit with bell-shaped flowers.
C. x *williamsii* 'Brigadoon' ♀ Small, dense upright shrub with semi-double blooms.
cultivation: Plant in autumn

in large pots of ericaceous compost. To protect the flowers from frost and thaw damage, position the plant away from full early morning sun, ideally in dappled shade. Water freely in growth. If the rootball dries out, flower buds will abort next spring.

Feed annually in late spring with a balanced liquid fertiliser. Top-dress in autumn with leaf-mould. Prune to shape after flowering. Scale insect may be troublesome.

Primula
Primrose
'Groeneken's Glory'
Rosette forming, evergreen perennial producing deeply veined leaves and saucer-shaped bluish pink flowers with a yellow eye.
height & spread: 15x25cm
P. vulgaris 'Pink Shades' Vibrant pink blooms.
P. vulgaris 'Rose Shades' Flowers are pinkish red.
cultivation: Plant primulas in early spring in a humus-rich compost and site in sun or light shade. Water moderately and apply a balanced liquid feed once flowering begins.

Remove faded flowers to prolong flowering period. Increase plants by dividing them after 2 years.

Ranunculus asiaticus
'Accolade Pink'
Tuberous perennial producing large, double, peony-like flowers on slender, branched stems above a ruff of foliage.
height & spread: 25x15cm
R. asiaticus 'Bloomingdale Pink Shades' Very large and

showy flowers.
cultivation: Plant out in early spring into a good-quality potting mix. Site in full sun. These cultivars will tolerate moderate frost but should be moved to a sheltered position if a cold spell is severe. Water moderately. No need to feed. Remove spent flowers. Plant tubers in autumn for spring flowers.

Tulipa aucheriana ♀
Tulip
Dwarf species tulip producing star-shaped flowers with a yellow eye.
height: 10cm
T. 'China Pink' Tall, stately, lily-like flowers with pointed reflexed petals.
height: 50cm
T. 'Peach Blossom' Semi-double, deep rose flowers.
height: 30cm
cultivation: Completely hardy. Plant bulbs in autumn in a loam-based compost 15cm deep. Site in sun or light shade out of wind. Water when growing; no need to feed. Deadhead to encourage growth of new bulbs.

Lift bulbs once foliage fades and store in a dry place; remove daughter bulbs and grow them on.

Summer

Antirrhinum majus
Snapdragon
'Ribbon Light Pink'
Tubular, two-lipped flowers carried in dense, upright spikes on bushy plants.
height & spread: 50x25cm
A. majus 'La Bella Rose' Open, rounded flowers of clear pink. Fragrant.

A. majus 'Chimes Pink' Yellow-throated flowers on bushy, dwarf plants.
height & spread: 20x20cm
cultivation: Plant out after the last frosts in a good-quality, free-draining potting mix. Site in sun or partial shade. Water freely while growing and apply a liquid tomato feed every 2 weeks. Pinch out tips of young plants for bushy growth, and cut off spent flower spikes.

Argyranthemum
Marguerite
'Vancouver' ♀
Vigorous evergreen sub-shrub with finely dissected, greyish green leaves. On a sunny patio, they will flower from early summer to late autumn. Pale pink, daisy-like flowers of 'Vancouver' have a central pompom.
height & spread: 60x30cm
A. 'Mary Cheek' ♀ Compact with pale pink pompom flowers.
A. 'Petite Pink' ♀ Compact in habit, silvery foliage and abundant pale pink flowers with a yellow eye.
height & spread: 30x30cm
cultivation: Plant in a good-quality, free-draining potting mix after frost has passed, and site in full sun. Water freely in summer and keep almost dry in winter to improve hardiness.

Feed fortnightly with a balanced liquid fertiliser. Cut off dead flower stalks.

Armeria juniperifolia
Thrift, sea pink
'Bevan's Variety' ♀
Evergreen perennial

forming dense cushions of narrow, linear leaves. The globular, dark pink flowerheads are held above the foliage on slender leafless stems.

height & spread: 5x15cm

A. 'Bee's Ruby' ♀ Taller with dark pink flowers.

A. maritima 'Vindictive' ♀ A much larger variety with deep, rose-pink flowers.

cultivation: Plant in spring to early summer in pots of John Innes No.2 with extra sand for good drainage. Site in full sun. Water moderately, avoiding overwetting the compost. Apply a balanced liquid feed monthly in growing season. Cut off faded flower stalks. Increase by dividing established clumps in early spring.

Catharanthus roseus
Madagascar periwinkle

Syn. *Vinca rosea*

Glossy-leaved perennial, usually grown as annual. The flowers have 5 satiny petals.

C. roseus does not tolerate temperatures below 7℃.

height & spread: 30x30cm

C. roseus 'Blush Cooler' Pale pink with a deep pink eye.

C. roseus 'Pacifica Coral' Pale pink.

cultivation: Plant out after last frosts in a moist, humus-rich, free-draining potting mixture. Site the containers in full sun.

During growing season water moderately and apply a balanced liquid feed once a month. Control growth and keep the plants bushy by pinching out tips. Plants may be trimmed back and overwintered in a well-heated greenhouse or conservatory.

Dianthus chinensis
Indian pink

'Raspberry Parfait'

Branching and compact perennial usually grown as an annual. Deep pink petals have a large crimson eye.

height & spread: 20x15cm

D. 'Ideal Fuchsia' Fuchsia pink flowers laced with paler patterning.

D. 'Princess Pink' Intense pink flowers.

cultivation: Plant out after last frosts in a good-quality potting mix. Position the pot where it will receive continuous sun.

Water moderately, applying a balanced liquid feed every 4 weeks. Deadhead to prolong flowering.

Diascia

'Twinkle' ♀

Upright perennial usually grown as an annual. Compact plants with profuse shell-like, five-lobed flowers borne in dense spikes above heart-shaped leaves. First flush appears in early summer and, if plant is trimmed back, new shoots appear which flower later.

height & spread: 30x20cm

D. 'Pink Queen' Loose spikes of rose-pink, yellow-eyed flowers.

D. 'Ruby Field' ♀ Free-flowering over a long season.

cultivation: Plant out after the last frosts in a good-quality potting mix and site in full sun. Do not allow the compost to dry out. Once established, feed every 2 weeks with a weak liquid fertiliser. Cut stems back after initial flowering. Diascia may be hardy in mild regions.

Fuchsia

'Pink Galore'

Free-flowering, trailing shrub producing double blooms with pink outer sepals and pale rose-pink inner petals.

height & spread: 20x30cm

F. 'Lady Thumb' ♀ Dwarf, upright shrub. Semi-double flowers have white inner petals with pink veins and pink outer sepals.

height & spread: 23x30cm

F. 'Rose of Denmark' Trailing in habit up to 40cm. Pink petals and sepals.

cultivation: Plant out hardened-off plants after last frosts. Plant in a good-quality potting mix, using a pot large enough to ensure a reasonable root run.

Site in sun or light shade. Water frequently, especially in dry spells, and apply a balanced liquid fertiliser every 3 weeks. Deadhead to prolong flowering.

In autumn, move plants into a cool shed or greenhouse. Water just often enough to prevent the roots from drying out.

In spring, begin watering again to restart the plants into growth. Watch for red spider mite and aphids.

Hydrangea macrophylla

'Parzifal' ♀

Compact deciduous shrub with glossy serrated leaves, and large mophead flowerheads of dark pink.

height & spread: 1.2x1m

H. macrophylla 'Ayesha' ♀ Lilac-like clusters of pale bluish pink flowers.

cultivation: Plant in autumn in a large container of moisture-retentive, humus-rich compost. Pink-flowered hydrangeas do not need ericaceous compost; in fact, if you plant 'Parzifal' in acid soil, it will produce deep blue flowers. Site in sun or partial shade with shelter from cold, drying winds.

Water generously while growing and apply liquid feed monthly. Top-dress annually in autumn with garden compost or leaf-mould. Leave spent flowerheads until spring, then prune back stems to a strong pair of buds.

Lavatera
Tree mallow

'Pink Frills'

Vigorous, semi-evergreen shrub with wide, funnel-shaped flowers.

height & spread: 90x60cm

L. trimestris 'Pink Beauty' Smaller, quick-growing hardy annual. Light pink flowers with darker veins; dark glossy leaves.

L. trimestris 'Salmon Beauty' Quick-growing hardy annual. Salmon-pink flowers with darker veins.

cultivation: Plant out in early summer in a light, free-draining compost in full sun. Avoid windy sites. Water freely and apply a balanced liquid feed every 2 weeks.

Lilium
Lily
Pink Perfection Group ♀
Bulbous perennial producing clusters of 5 to 8 heavily scented, pendulous pink blooms.
height: 1.2m
L. 'Journey's End' Pink petals with white margins. This lily is unscented.
L. 'Star Gazer' Bears heavily scented, star-shaped, upward-facing flowers.
height: 90cm
cultivation: Plant bulbs in autumn at a depth of 3 times their own height. Use John Innes No.2, putting a good layer of crocks in the bottom of the pot. Select a sheltered position in full sun. Water freely while growing and give a high potash feed once a month.

Store lily bulbs over winter in pots, or lift them and store in boxes of damp sand in a cool dry place.

You can increase bulbs by removing their outer scales in autumn and growing them in trays of compost. Lily beetle may be a problem.

Lobelia erinus
'Rosamund'
Bushy, mound-forming annual with tiny leaves on slender stems. Fan-shaped flowers are bright pink with a white eye.
height & spread: 15x10cm
L. erinus 'Rose Fountains' Vigorous trailing habit.
cultivation: Plant out after the last frosts in a good-quality potting mix. Site the container in sun or light shade. Do not allow the compost to dry out.

Apply a liquid tomato feed every 2 to 3 weeks. Clip plants occasionally to encourage further flowering.

Lobularia maritima
Sweet alyssum
Syn. *Alyssum maritimum*
'Pastel Carpet'
Low-growing, compact, easy to grow annual. Tiny, 4-petalled flowers borne in profusion throughout summer in dense, fragrant clusters. 'Pastel Carpet' seed mix produces white, pink and violet flowers.
height & spread: 10x20cm
L. maritima 'Rosie O'Day' Rose-pink, low-growing.
L. maritima 'Wonderland Pastel Pink' Pale pink.
cultivation: Grow plants in a moderately fertile, free-draining compost in full sun. Water freely and feed every month with a high potash fertiliser, such as liquid tomato feed.

Clip after the first flush to encourage further flowering. You can sow seed directly into the container in late spring.

Nicotiana x sanderae
Tobacco plant
'Havana Apple Blossom'
One of the Havana Series, 'Havana Apple Blossom' is an upright, branching annual with loose clusters of tubular flowers, flared at the mouth. Only slightly fragrant. The stems and oval leaves are sticky.
height & spread: 30x15cm
N. x sanderae 'Merlin Salmon Pink' Dwarf annual with soft pink flowers.
cultivation: Plant out once the danger of frost has

passed in a good-quality, moist but free-draining compost.

Site in sun or shade. Water liberally and apply a liquid tomato feed every 2 weeks. Deadhead regularly.
NB Nicotianas are poisonous.

Penstemon
'Hewell Pink Bedder' ♀
Short-lived perennial with oval, pointed leaves and tall spikes of bright reddish pink tubular flowers.
height & spread: 50x30cm
P. 'Apple Blossom' ♀ The pale pink flowers have white throats.
P. 'Hidcote Pink' ♀ Pink flowers with white and dark pink streaks.
cultivation: Plant in spring into pots of John Innes No.2 and site in sheltered, sunny spot. Keep well watered and feed every fortnight with a balanced liquid fertiliser. Cut off spent flower spikes to encourage further flowers.

Rosa
Patio rose
'Queen Mother' ♀
Dwarf, cluster-flowered patio rose bearing soft, flat, pink, scented blooms.
height & spread: 35x35cm
R. 'Judy Fischer' Miniature rose, with slightly scented, tiny dark pink flowers.
cultivation: Plant in spring in a fertile, humus-rich compost and site in full sun. Water freely and apply a balanced liquid feed every 3 weeks throughout spring and summer. Add a layer of well-rotted manure as a

mulch each spring.

Prune annually in early spring, cutting back main stems to about 20cm from the base. Cut off damaged shoots.

Deadhead regularly to prolong flowering.

Susceptible to pests and diseases, including aphids, black spot, powdery mildew and rust.

Verbena x hybrida
'Quartz Rose'
Vigorous, mound-forming half-hardy dwarf perennial, usually grown as an annual, with large, domed heads of bright pink flowers.
height & spread: 20x30cm
V. x hybrida 'Sissinghurst' ♀ Deep pink flowers borne on trailing plants.
cultivation: Plant out after the last frosts in a good-quality potting mix. Site the containers in full sun.

Water freely, especially in dry spells. Apply a balanced liquid feed every month. Deadheading will help to prolong flowering.

Zinnia
'Short Stuff Coral'
Low-growing, floriferous annual with large, double, soft pink flowers.
height & spread: 20x20cm
Z. 'Dreamland Pink' Bright pink blooms.
Z. 'Peter Pan Princess' Large pale pink flowers on dwarf plants, up to 10cm high.
cultivation: Plant out after the last frosts into a free-draining compost. Site in full sun. Water moderately and apply a liquid tomato feed every 2 weeks. Deadhead to prolong

flowering. Stagger sowing for continuous flowering into autumn.

Autumn

Callistephus chinensis
China aster
'Milady Rose'♀
Erect, bushy, fast-growing annual with large, fully double, chrysanthemum-like flowers of rose pink.
height & spread: 25x25cm
C. chinensis 'Asteroid Rose' Abundant semi-double flowers to 10cm across.
C. chinensis 'Compliment Salmon Pink' Double flowers on strong, upright stems.
height & spread: 65x20cm
cultivation: Plant out after the last frosts in a good-quality potting mix. Site in full sun. Water moderately and feed every 2 weeks once established using a balanced liquid fertiliser.

Taller varieties may need staking. Deadhead to prolong flowering. Sow seed in early spring. Repeated sowing in early summer guarantees autumn-flowering plants. Prone to callistephus wilt.

Crinum x powellii♀
Bulbous, deciduous perennial with long, arching strap-shaped leaves. Up to ten large trumpet-shaped flowers borne in umbels (rounded flowerheads), at the top of sturdy flower stems.
height & spread: 90x60cm
cultivation: Plant in spring with the neck of the bulb just above soil level. Use John Innes No.2 with added sharp sand. Site in a sheltered, sunny position.

Water freely in growth but keep almost dry in winter. Apply a diluted tomato fertiliser every month from spring to summer. Remove spent blooms. Repot bulbs only when essential.

Nerine bowdenii ♀
This bulbous perennial produces loose clusters of up to eight fragile, slender-petalled, rose-pink flowers.
height: 45cm
N. bowdenii 'Pink Triumph' Has deep pink flowers.
cultivation: Plant in spring in pots of John Innes No.2, at a depth of 10cm. Site in a sheltered sunny spot. Keep warm and dry during summer dormancy, and begin watering freely as growth commences in late summer. Apply a balanced liquid feed as the flower buds open.

A dry winter mulch will protect against extreme winter cold. Divide congested clumps during dormancy. Otherwise avoid disturbing the bulbs.

Winter

Cyclamen coum♀
Tuberous perennial with rounded dark green leaves marked with silver pattern. Flowers with swept-back petals are held on upright stalks above the rounded unlobed leaves.
height & spread: 7.5x10cm
C. persicum 'Miracle Rose' A large-flowered, scented cultivar suitable for use under glass, or outdoors in only the mildest areas.
height & spread: 15x15cm
cultivation: Use humus-rich, well-drained compost.

Plant tubers of *C. coum* in late summer at a depth of about 5cm. *C. persicum* cultivars are usually bought in flower and can be planted out immediately in mild, sheltered areas (such as window boxes in urban areas). While growing, water cyclamen moderately, taking care to avoid the crown, and apply a balanced liquid fertiliser when in flower. Reduce watering as the leaves wither after flowering.

Keep tubers of *C. coum* just moist in summer. *C. persicum* cultivars need a 2 to 3 month period of dry dormancy. Water to restart growth in early autumn. Vine weevil may damage tubers.

Erica x darleyensis
Heath, heather
'Jenny Porter'♀
Compact, bushy evergreen shrub with small, bottle-green needle-like leaves and pale pink, bell-shaped flowers carried in clusters at the tips of the shoots.
height & spread: 40x40cm
E. x darleyensis 'Furzey'♀ Lilac-pink flowers and pink-tipped spring foliage.
E. x darleyensis 'Ghost Hills'♀ Bright green foliage is cream-tipped in spring.
cultivation: Plant in autumn in pots of humus-rich compost (it does not need ericaceous compost). Site in full sun. Water freely and apply a weak liquid feed every 4 weeks. Clip flower spikes back once they are past their best. Botrytis (grey mould) may develop in warm, humid conditions.

Gaultheria mucronata
Syn. *Pernettya mucronata*
'Pink Pearl'♀
Woody, branching evergreen shrub with dense clusters of round, clear pink berries persisting through winter.
height & spread: 75x45cm
G. mucronata 'Mulberry Wine'♀ Mauve-pink berries.
G. mucronata 'Seashell'♀ Pale pink berries.
cultivation: Plant in autumn into ericaceous compost. Site in full sun or partial shade. Water frequently, preferably with rainwater. Apply a liquid tomato feed monthly from spring to late summer. Prune to shape in winter. For berries the next year, a male plant must be grown nearby.

Red flowers

Spring

Bellis perennis
'Tasso Deep Rose'
Fully double pompom flowers held on short stems above mats of bright green leaf rosettes. They are hardy perennials but are often grown as biennials because flower size and quality decline with each flowering.
height & spread: 15x10cm
B. perennis 'Galaxy Red' Semi-double flowers with a yellow eye.
cultivation: Plant in autumn in free-draining, humus-rich compost. Site in full sun or partial shade. Water plants moderately and apply a balanced liquid

feed once the buds form. Deadhead to prolong flowering. Increase by dividing every 2 years.

Camellia japonica
'Coquettii'♀

Slow-growing, compact, erect evergreen shrub with glossy dark foliage and double, deep red flowers.

height & spread: 2.4x1.2m
C. japonica 'Miss Charleston'♀ Neat, upright shrub with large, deep red semi-double flowers with golden stamens.

cultivation: Plant in autumn in a large pot of ericaceous compost. To protect flowers from frost/thaw damage, position plant where it will not be exposed to full early morning sun. Camellias grow best in dappled shade. Water freely while growing: if the rootball becomes dry in summer the flower buds will abort the following spring.

Feed annually in late spring with a balanced liquid fertiliser. Top-dress in autumn with leaf-mould. Prune to shape after flowering. Scale insect may be troublesome.

Erysimum cheiri
Syn. *Cheiranthus cheiri*
Wallflower
'Ruby Gem'

Biennial sub-shrub with lance-shaped leaves and clusters of sweetly scented, 4-petalled flowers.

height & spread: 30x25cm
E. cheiri 'Scarlet Bedder' Slightly shorter variety.

cultivation: Plant bedding wallflowers in early autumn in a free-draining,

neutral or slightly alkaline compost and site in a sheltered sunny position. Water moderately. Feeding is unnecessary.

Pinch out the growing tips to encourage bushiness, and trim after flowering to encourage further blooms.

Ranunculus asiaticus
'Accolade Red Shades'

Striking tuberous perennial producing large, fully double, peony-like flowers in a range of red shades.

height & spread: 25x15cm
R. asiaticus 'Bloomingdale Red Shades' Very large showy flowers in a range from coppery to blood red.

cultivation: Plant out in early spring in a good-quality, moist, potting mix. Site the pots in a sunny position. They will tolerate moderate frost, but should be moved to a sheltered position if a cold spell is severe or prolonged.

Water moderately. Feeding is unnecessary. Deadhead any spent flowers to encourage further flowering.

Tulipa
'Oxford'♀

Large scarlet flowers flushed inside with blood red, and brilliant red, held at the top of tall stems.

height: 50cm
T. 'Plaisir'♀ Shorter variety. Carmine with pale sulphur at the base. Striking maroon stripes on leaves.

height: 15cm
cultivation: Plant bulbs from early to late autumn, 15cm deep in free-draining loam-based compost.

Apply potash-rich fertiliser in late winter and water well while growing. Site the pot in a sunny, sheltered spot, out of the wind. Deadhead and keep moist while growing.

Increase by removing daughter bulbs and growing them on. Prone to tulip fire, a fungal disease.

Summer

Abutilon
Flowering maple
'Ashford Red'♀

Fast-growing, twiggy shrub with heart-shaped, serrated leaves and bell-shaped hanging flowers.

height & spread: 90x60cm
A. 'Cannington Carol'♀ Dwarf plant whose leaves are mottled with yellow.

height & spread: 45x45cm
cultivation: Grow in pots of John Innes No.3 with added leaf-mould. Select a sunny, sheltered site. While growing, water freely and feed monthly. Overwinter plants under glass, and in spring prune back by about two-thirds of the previous year's growth.

Alonsoa
warscewiczii♀
Mask flower

Fast-growing, branching annual with glossy oval leaves and abundant small scarlet flowers borne on upright, dark red stems.

height & spread: 40x25cm
cultivation: Plant out after last frosts in free-draining compost. Site in full sun in a sheltered position or grow in a conservatory.

Water moderately and apply a balanced liquid

feed every month during the growing season. Pinch out tips of young plants to promote branching. It is susceptible to aphids and to powdery mildew during dry spells.

Amaranthus caudatus
Love-lies-bleeding

Bushy half-hardy annual with pale green leaves and long, drooping tassel-like clusters of tiny blood-red flowers.

height & spread: 60x40cm
A. cruentus 'Foxtail' (syn *A. paniculatus*) Has upright flower spikes and bronze-tinted foliage.

cultivation: Plant out after last frosts in a humus-rich compost. Site in full sun and support taller plants with stakes, especially those in windy areas.

Water freely in summer and apply a balanced liquid feed every month. Pinch out tips of young *A. cruentus* plants to encourage bushiness.

Antirrhinum majus
Snapdragon
'Coronette Crimson'♀

Fragrant, tubular, two-lipped flowers carried in dense, upright spikes on bushy, branching plants. Usually grown as annual.

height & spread: 50x25cm
A. majus 'La Bella Red' Spikes of open, rounded, fragrant flowers.
A. majus 'Chimes Red' Rich red flowers are borne on dwarf, bushy plants.

height & spread: 15x15cm
cultivation: Plant out in spring after last frosts in a good-quality potting mix. Site in sun or partial

shade. Water freely in growth and apply a liquid tomato feed every 2 weeks. Remove spent flower spikes to encourage repeat flowering. Plants may suffer from rust.

Arctotis x hybrida
African daisy
'Flame'
Orange-red, daisy-like flowers are carried on long stems above silvery green lobed leaves.
height & spread: 45x30cm
cultivation: Grow in pots of John Innes No.2 and site in full sun because the flowers close up in dull weather. Drought-tolerant but performs better with moderate watering. Feed once a month with a balanced liquid fertiliser. Deadhead to prolong flowering. Susceptible to grey mould and slugs in damp weather.

Capsicum annuum
Chilli pepper
'Redskin'
Compact annual producing numerous small, bell-pepper fruits to 5cm long. Go from green or white to bright red as they mature.
height & spread: 15x10cm
C. annuum 'Treasures Red' Produces small, conical, upward-pointing fruits.
height & spread: 30x30cm
cultivation: Plant in humus-rich compost and site in a sunny, sheltered position once the risk of frost has passed. Support will be needed. Water freely while growing and give a liquid tomato fertiliser every 2 weeks until the fruits begin to colour. Pinch out tips of

young plants to encourage bushiness. They can be susceptible to red spider mite and aphids.

Dahlia
'Bednall Beauty'
Fast-growing, dwarf, bushy, tuberous perennial with bronze foliage and double scarlet flowers.
height & spread: 30x20cm
D. 'Ellen Houston' ♀ Striking plant with purple foliage and dark red flowers.
D. 'Figaro Red Shades' Yellow eyed semi-double flowers.
height & spread: 50x30cm
cultivation: Plant out after the last frosts in a free-draining, humus-rich compost. Site in full sun. Water freely while growing and apply balanced liquid feed every 2 weeks. Deadhead to encourage more shoots and flowers.

In late autumn, lift tubers, trim dead stems and store upside down in boxes of dry sand in frost-free greenhouse or shed. Increase by division of tubers in early spring. Dahlias are prone to powdery mildew.

Gaillardia
Blanket flower
'Dazzler' ♀
Short-lived, bushy annual with daisy-like flowers. Tips of petals are yellow.
height & spread: 60x20cm
G. 'Dwarf Goblin' Similar flowers on shorter plants.
height & spread: 25x15cm
cultivation: Plant in spring in a free-draining compost and position in full sun. Taller flowers may need staking for support. Water moderately and apply a

liquid tomato feed monthly in the growing season. Deadhead to prolong flowering. Divide in autumn to increase.

Lotus berthelotii ♀
Parrot's beak
Trailing evergreen sub-shrub with needle-like, silvery green leaves and a curved, beak-like flowers.
height & spread: 20x45cm
cultivation: Grow in pots of John Innes No.2 with extra grit. Plant in a basket so that stems can trail down.

Position in full sun in a sheltered position. Flowering may disappoint in poor summers. Water moderately while growing, giving a balanced liquid feed monthly. Overwinter in a warm greenhouse or conservatory, keeping compost almost dry.

Lycopersicon lycopersicum
Tomato
'Tumbler'
Specifically bred for containers, this trailing annual bears dozens of tasty cherry tomatoes from midsummer to autumn.
height & spread: 60x45cm
L. lycopersicum 'Red Alert' Bushy, upright annual produces cherry tomatoes.
height & spread: 50x40cm
cultivation: Plant out after the last frosts in a moisture-retentive, humus-rich compost. Site in full sun in a sheltered position. Water freely while growing (dry spells cause the fruits to split) and apply a liquid tomato feed once a week.

Neither variety mentioned here requires

pinching or staking. Remove ripe or spoiling fruits regularly. Tomatoes are prone to various moulds, rots and viruses.

Mimulus
Monkey flower
'Whitecroft Scarlet' ♀
Open, trumpet-shaped flowers are borne in profusion on this low-growing, bushy annual or short-lived perennial.
height & spread: 10x15cm
M. 'Mystic Scarlet' Compact and free-flowering.
height & spread: 15x15cm
cultivation: Plant out in late spring in a humus-rich, moisture-retentive compost. Site in light shade. Do not allow the compost to dry out. Apply a balanced liquid fertiliser every 4 weeks.

Nicotiana x sanderae
Tobacco plant
'Saratoga Red'
Upright, branching annual with loose clusters of slightly fragrant, tubular flowers. Leaves and stems are sticky.
height & spread: 30x15cm
N. x sanderae 'Havana Red' Bright crimson flowers.
cultivation: Plant out after the last frosts in a moist but free-draining potting mix, in sun or partial shade. Water liberally and apply a liquid tomato feed every 2 weeks. Deadhead regularly.

Pelargonium
Geranium
'Caroline Schmidt' ♀
Erect and bushy zonal pelargonium with silvery white margins to leaves

and large, rounded clusters of double scarlet flowers.

height & spread: 45x30cm
P. 'Ann Hoysted'♀ Upright, bushy, regal pelargonium bearing large clusters of crimson flowers whose upper petals are flushed black-red.

height & spread: 45x30cm
P. 'Rote Mini-cascade' Trailing, ivy-leaved pelargonium bears open clusters of small, deep red starry flowers above glossy deep green leaves.

height & spread: 10x45cm
cultivation: Plant out after last frosts in a good-quality compost. Site in full sun. Ivy-leaved pelargoniums are good in hanging baskets.

Water freely while growing but sparingly in winter. In summer, fertilise with a balanced liquid feed every 3 weeks. Deadhead regularly and break off yellowing leaves.

Lift plants before first frosts and store almost dry over winter in frost-free shed or greenhouse.

Rosa
Patio rose
'Red Ace'
Bushy and upright dwarf evergreen shrub with clusters of fragrant, velvety flowers.

height & spread: 40x35cm
R. 'Boy's Brigade' Red flowers with white eyes. Long flowering season.
R. 'Little Buckaroo' Crimson flowers with white eyes and golden stamens.
cultivation: Plant in spring into a fertile, humus-rich compost and site in full sun. Water freely and

apply a balanced liquid feed every 3 weeks throughout spring and summer. Add a layer of well-rotted manure as a mulch each spring.

Prune annually in early spring, cutting back main stems to 20-25cm from the ground. Remove dead or damaged shoots. Dead-heading roses regularly will prolong flowering.

Roses are susceptible to black spot, powdery mildew and rose rust, so need regular spraying.

Salvia splendens
'Fury'
Bushy annual with dense spikes of long tubular scarlet flowers emerging from conspicuous red bracts and toothed leaves.

height & spread: 25x20cm
S. splendens 'Salsa Scarlet Bicolor' Tips of petals are white and the bracts are streaked with white.
S. splendens 'Scarlet King' Intense scarlet flowers and very dark green foliage.
cultivation: Plant out after last frosts in a good-quality, moist, but free-draining compost. Site in full sun or light shade. Water liberally while growing and apply a liquid tomato feed every 2 weeks. Remove all faded flower spikes.

Tropaeolum majus
Nasturtium
'Hermine Grashoff'♀
Fast-growing annual with rounded leaves and double, scarlet flowers.

height & spread: 1.2x1.2m
T. majus 'Empress of India' Dwarf plant with bushy, semi-double flowers,

purplish foliage.

height & spread: 30x45cm
T. majus 'Scarlet Gleam' Has velvety, semi-double flowers and a trailing habit.
cultivation: Grow in John Innes No.1 (a richer compost will encourage leaf growth at the expense of flowers). Site in sun or partial shade. Water well until established; after this nasturtiums are fairly drought-tolerant. Support scramblers or allow them to trail. Sow seed in pots in spring. Prone to blackfly.

Verbena
'Lawrence Johnson'♀
Bushy and mound-forming perennial, usually grown as annual, bearing brilliant scarlet flowers held in large, domed clusters.

height & spread: 25x30cm
V. x hybrida 'Quartz Scarlet' White-eyed red flowers are borne on mound-forming, vigorous plants.
cultivation: Plant out after the last frosts in a good-quality potting mix. Taller varieties will need staking for support. Site in full sun.

Water the plants well, especially during dry spells. Apply a balanced liquid fertiliser every month. Deadhead regularly to encourage further displays of flowers.

Autumn

Callistephus chinensis
China aster
'Pommax Deep Red'
Erect, bushy, fast-growing dwarf annual bears yellow-centred chrysanthemum-like blooms.

height & spread: 25x25cm
C. chinensis 'Milady Scarlet'♀ Shorter-stemmed fully double flowers can be up to 10cm across, on a dwarf plant.
C. chinensis 'Matsumo Red' Tall semi-double flowers with a yellow eye.
height & spread: 75x40cm
cultivation: Plant out in spring in a good-quality potting mix. Site the pot in full sun. Taller varieties may need staking.

Water moderately and fertilise every 2 weeks once established, using a balanced liquid feed. Deadhead to prolong flowering. Prone to callistephus wilt (a soil-borne disease) and to attack by aphids.

Canna
Canna lily
'Lucifer'
Tropical-looking rhizomatous perennial producing tall spikes of iris-like flowers. The red petals have yellow margins. The large, oval, slightly bluish green leaves spiral up the stem. Canna lilies make an excellent tall feature in a large container.

height: Up to 60cm
C. 'Endeavour' Bluish green foliage and iris-like flowers.
height: Up to 1.5m
C. 'King Humbert' Another tall lily with purple leaves and bright red flowers.
height: Up to 1.5m
cultivation: Plant rhizomes in large pots of humus-rich, free-draining compost in late winter or early spring. Grow in frost-free conditions until early summer. Pots can then be

moved outside to a sheltered sunny spot.

Water liberally and apply a tomato fertiliser every 4 weeks. Deadhead to prolong flowering.

After the first frost blackens the foliage, lift the rhizomes, trim off any dead growth and store in slightly moist compost in a frost-free place over winter.

Winter

Cyclamen persicum
'Miracle Scarlet'
Tuberous perennial with heart-shaped, silver-patterned leaves. Scented flowers with swept-back petals held on upright stalks above foliage.
height & spread: 10x10cm
C. persicum 'Laser Scarlet' Bright, intense red flowers.
cultivation: Plant out in winter in a humus rich, free-draining compost. Site in full sun in a very sheltered position, such as a window box. In all but the mildest areas, *C. persicum* cultivars should be grown in a porch or conservatory.

While growing, water moderately, avoiding the crown. Apply a balanced liquid feed while in flower. Reduce watering as leaves wither after flowering, and keep dry for 2 to 3 months in summer. Resume watering in early autumn. Vine weevils may damage the corms.

Skimmia japonica
'Nymans' ♀
Evergreen female shrub with red-tinged stalks bearing profuse, bright red

berries throughout winter. These are preceded by clusters of small off-white flowers.
height & spread: 75x75cm
S. japonica 'Veitchii' (syn. 'Foremanii') Vigorous upright female plant with clusters of scarlet berries.
height & spread: Up to 1.5x1.5m
cultivation: Plant in autumn into pots of John Innes No.3 with added organic matter such as leaf-mould. Site in partial to deep shade. Keep the compost moist and apply a balanced liquid feed monthly from spring to late summer. For these female skimmias to continue producing flowers and berries, a male plant, such as *S. japonica* 'Fragrans' ♂, must be grown nearby.

Orange flowers

Spring

Epimedium x warleyense
Evergreen perennial. Cross-shaped flowers and heart-shaped leaves flush red in spring and autumn.
height & spread: 40x40cm
E. x versicolor 'Cupreum' Coppery orange flowers.
cultivation: Plant in autumn in humus-rich, free-draining compost, in light shade. Water freely while growing and apply a liquid feed monthly. Mulch with leaf-mould in autumn. Remove the old foliage in spring to allow the new growth to show through.

Erysimum cheiri
Syn. *Cheiranthus cheiri*
Wallflower
'Orange Bedder'
A biennial sub-shrub with lance-shaped leaves and clusters of sweetly scented, 4-petalled flowers.
height & spread: 25x25cm
E. hieraciifolium ♀ (syn. *E. x allionii*) Tall species with brilliant orange flowers with hairs on the backs of the petals.
height & spread: 50x30cm
cultivation: Plant in early autumn into free-draining, neutral to alkaline compost and site in full sun. Water moderately. No need to feed. Pinch out growing tips to encourage bushiness. Prone to club root and root rot.

Ranunculus asiaticus
'Accolade Tangerine'
Tuberous perennial producing large, peony or poppy-like flowers on compact plants.
height & spread: 25x15cm
R. asiaticus 'Bloomingdale Orange Bi-colour' Bears orange flowers with petals shading to white at base.
cultivation: Plant out in early spring into a good-quality potting mix. Site in full sun. These cultivars will tolerate light frost but should be moved to a sheltered position if cold weather is severe. Water moderately. No need to feed. Remove spent flowers.

Tulipa
Tulip
'Prinses Irene' ♀
Bulb producing large, cup-shaped flowers with

purple feathering on the outer petals.
height: 30cm
T. 'Orange Banquet' ♀ Deep orange cup-shaped flowers with a pale yellow base.
T. 'Orange Favourite' The flowers have finely and irregularly cut petals.
height: 50cm
cultivation: In autumn, plant bulbs 10cm deep in a loam-based compost. Place the bulbs close together. Site in sun or shade in a sheltered position out of the wind. In growth, water moderately. Remove the spent flowers.

Summer

Calendula officinalis
Pot marigold
'Fiesta Gitana' ♀
Dense, branching, dwarf plant with scented leaves and semi-double, daisy-like flowers.
height & spread: 25x20cm
C. officinalis 'Orange King' Taller with double flowers.
height & spread: 45x30cm
cultivation: Plant in spring in John Innes No.1, to promote flowers rather than foliage, and site in sun or shade. Water moderately but do not feed. Deadhead to prolong period of flowering.

Cuphea cyanea
Evergreen sub-shrub with glossy oval leaves and green-tipped, orangey red, tubular flowers.
height & spread: 60x60cm
C. ignea ♀ Cigar plant. The scarlet tubular flowers have white tips, that look like ash on cigars.

cultivation: Plant in a good-quality potting mix and place in a sunny sheltered position. Water freely while growing, applying a balanced liquid feed every 3 weeks. Pinch out growing tips to encourage bushiness. Overwinter in a warm conservatory.

Dahlia
'Figaro Orange Shades'
Bushy and fast-growing dwarf tuberous perennial producing a mass of semi-double orange flowers with a yellow eye.
height & spread: 30x20cm
D. 'Inflammation' Produces abundant smaller blooms.
cultivation: Plant out after the last frosts in a free-draining, fertile, humus-rich compost. Site in full sun. Water freely while growing and apply a liquid feed every 2 weeks.

Deadhead to prolong flowering. In late autumn, once frost has blackened the foliage, lift the tubers, trim off dead stems, and store upside down in boxes of dry sand in a frost-free greenhouse or conservatory.

Increase by seed or division of tubers in early spring. These plants are prone to powdery mildew.

Diascia
'Blackthorn Apricot' ♀
Upright perennial grown as an annual. Compact plant with heart-shaped leaves and loose spikes of pale apricot flowers.
height & spread: 20x40cm
D. 'Joyce's Choice' ♀ Soft apricot-coloured blooms.
cultivation: Plant out after

the last frosts in a good-quality potting mix. Site in full sun. Keep the compost moist at all times. Feed every fortnight with a weak, balanced liquid fertiliser. Cut back after flowering to encourage a second flush.

Eccremocarpus scaber ♀
Chilean glory vine
Fast-growing perennial climber with clusters of long tubular flowers and dark green leaves. Climbs by means of tendrils.
height & spread: 3x1m
cultivation: Plant out in late spring in a light, free-draining potting mix. Select a sheltered site in full sun. Provide a trellis or wigwam support for the climbing stems. Water freely while growing, applying a balanced liquid feed every month. Keep almost dry in winter, adding a deep, dry mulch to improve hardiness. If frost kills top growth, plant usually resprouts in spring.

Gazania
'Cookei' ♀
Low-growing bushy perennial with grey foliage and daisy-like orange flowers with slate-blue ring around a yellow centre.
height & spread: 25x25cm
G. 'Daybreak Bright Orange' Brown ring around yellow eye and silvery leaves.
G. 'Kiss Bronze' Particularly useful as it blooms well even in dull weather, which causes many gazania flowers to close.
cultivation: Plant in a sunny spot in early summer in

free-draining compost. Water moderately until established; then fairly drought-tolerant. Feeding is unnecessary. Overwinter in a frost-free greenhouse.

Helianthus annuus
Sunflower
'Teddy Bear'
Fast-growing annual with large, fully double, orange-yellow pompom flowers.
height: 60cm
H. annuus 'Sunspot' Single flowers, to 20cm across, with a yellow-green eye.
cultivation: Grow in free-draining compost in a sunny, sheltered position. Water freely while growing and feed fortnightly. The short varieties mentioned here do not require staking unless the site is exposed. Sow seed in the pot.

Hemerocallis fulva
Day lily
'Flore Pleno'
Evergreen perennial with strap-shaped leaves and double lily-like flowers.
height & spread: 90x90cm
H. 'Bertie Ferris' Herbaceous perennial with apricot flowers.
height: 45cm
H. 'Outrageous' Coppery orange flowers with dark brown eyes.
cultivation: Plant in spring in large pots of John Innes No.3 with added organic matter such as leaf-mould. Site in full sun, (NB they tolerate windy sites). Water freely while growing, and apply a balanced liquid fertiliser every fortnight from spring until the buds form. Divide clumps every 2 years or so, in spring.

Impatiens walleriana
Busy lizzie
'Accent Apricot'
Low-growing, bushy perennial usually grown as an annual. Free-flowering with soft orange blooms and fleshy, wavy-edged, oval leaves.
height & spread: 20x20cm
I. walleriana 'Tempo Orange' Bright orange flowers.
I. walleriana 'Mega Orange Star' Salmon-orange flowers with radial white stripes.
cultivation: Plant out in spring after the last frosts. Busy lizzies do well in sun or light shade. Water freely while growing, applying a balanced liquid fertiliser every 3 weeks. Pinch out tips to promote bushiness.

Lilium
Lily
'Enchantment' ♀
Bulb producing up to 12 upward-facing, bright orange, star-shaped flowers, each 10cm in diameter, which have black-spotted throats.
height: 90cm
L. bulbiferum var. *croceum* ♀ Large, bowl-shaped blooms.
L. 'Orange Pixie' Up to 5 upward-facing, starry flowers on short, sturdy stems.
height: 50cm
cultivation: Plant bulbs in autumn at a depth of 3 times their own height. Use John Innes No.2 and put a good layer of crocks in the bottom of the pot. Site in a sheltered position in partial shade. Water freely while growing and give a high potash feed

once a month. Overwinter bulbs in pots, or store in boxes of damp sand in a cool, dry place. Remove outer scales of bulbs and grow them on.

Mimulus
Monkey flower
'Highland Orange'
Trumpet-shaped flowers, loved by bees, on a bushy, often short-lived perennial.
height & spread: 25x25cm
M. 'Magic Orange' Bright orange flowers.
M. 'Magic Peach' Soft, peachy orange flowers.
cultivation: Plant in humus-rich, moisture-retentive compost in light shade. Apply a balanced liquid fertiliser every month.

Nemesia strumosa
'Orange Prince'
Bushy, erect annual bearing abundant 2-lipped, vivid orange flowers.
height & spread: 25x15cm
cultivation: Plant out in spring after the last frosts into a moisture-retentive compost. Position the pots in a sheltered, sunny site.

Water frequently in dry weather and apply a liquid tomato feed every 2 weeks. Cut back hard after first flush of blooms for further flowering.

Sanvitalia procumbens
Creeping zinnia
Mat-forming annual with bright yellow-orange, daisy-like flowers with a black eye.
height & spread: 15x30cm
S. procumbens 'Irish Eyes' Golden-orange petals surround a greenish eye.

cultivation: Plant in late spring in free-draining, preferably light compost. Position at the edge of the container so that the stems can trail down. Site in full sun. Water moderately. Feed monthly with a balanced liquid fertiliser.

Tagetes patula
French marigold
'Aurora Orange'
Fast-growing upright annual with aromatic, divided leaves and large double flowers.
height & spread: 20x15cm
T. patula 'Alamo Flame' Double flowers, the outer petals are coppery red.
T. patula 'Orange Boy' Compact and free-flowering.
T. erecta 'Inca Orange' African marigold with fully double, pompom flowers on erect plants.
height & spread: 35x20cm
cultivation: Plant out after the last frosts in John Innes No.2 and site in full sun. Water moderately, more frequently during dry spells, and apply balanced liquid feed every 2 weeks. Deadhead occasionally to prolong flowering. French marigolds are prone to attack by slugs and snails.

Thunbergia alata
Black-eyed Susan
Fast-growing, annual climber with twining stems and black centred, pale orange flowers.
height & spread: 1.5mx25cm
cultivation: Plant out after the last frosts into a free-draining compost. Site in full sun. Water freely and

apply balanced liquid feed every 2 weeks. Provide support for the twining stems, such as trellis or wires against a wall.

Zinnia
'Short Stuff Orange'
Low-growing, free-flowering annual with double, bright orange flowers up to 5cm across.
height & spread: 20x20cm
Z. haageana (syn. *Z. mexicana*) 'Orange Star' Has single, daisy-like blooms.
Z. 'Peter Pan Orange' Very compact dwarf plant with large double flowers.
cultivation: Plant out after the last frosts into a good-quality potting mix in full sun. Water freely while growing; feed every 2 weeks. Deadheading regularly will help to prolong flowering.

Autumn

Canna
Canna lily
'Wyoming'
Exotic, tropical-looking, rhizomatous perennial is half-hardy in Britain. Bears striking gladiolus-like flowers with frilly tangerine petals on tall spikes. Broad, oval leaves are brownish purple.
height & spread: 1.5mx50cm
C. 'Striata' Pale green leaves with bright yellow veins.
cultivation: Plant rhizomes in large pots of humus-rich compost in early spring. Grow on in frost-free conditions until early summer. Pots can then be moved outside to a

sheltered sunny spot. Water liberally and apply a tomato fertiliser every 4 weeks. Remove the spent flowers.

After the first frost blackens the foliage, lift the rhizomes and store in slightly damp compost in a frost-free shed or greenhouse over winter. Increase by division of rhizomes in early spring.

Pyracantha
Firethorn
'Golden Charmer'
Hardy evergreen shrub bears long-lasting berries in brilliant golden-orange. Upright at first, branches arch over as plant ages.
height & spread: 1.5x1.2m
P. 'Navaho' Small reddish orange berries.
height & spread: 1x1.2m
P. 'Orange Glow' ♀ Upright shrub; bearing deep orange berries.
height & spread: 1.8x1.8m
cultivation: Plant in humus-rich compost and site in sun or shade. Water moderately and feed monthly. Support with trellis or wires if grown against a wall.

Tropaeolum tuberosum
Perennial, deciduous climber with five-lobed, grey-green leaves and trumpet-shaped, orange-red flowers.
height & spread: 1.2x1.2m
cultivation: Plant tubers 15cm deep in spring. Use a humus-rich compost. Site in sun or partial shade. Ideally the container should be in shade and the stems in the sun. Water

freely while growing and apply a balanced liquid feed monthly. Provide support, such as trellis, for the twining stems, or allow the plant to ramble through another shrub.

In very cold areas move pot inside after frost has killed off top growth. It can be increased by dividing tubers in early spring.

Winter

Viola x wittrockiana
Winter pansy
'Universal Orange'♀
Low-growing perennial, grown as annual, with large, round, clear orange flowers produced during mild spells through winter.
height & spread: 16x20cm
V. x *wittrockiana* 'Turbo Orange Blotch' Brown blotch in centre of each flower.
cultivation: Plant in autumn and site in sun or shade. Water in dry spells. Deadhead regularly to prolong flowering. Loved by slugs and snails.

Yellow flowers

Spring

Aurinia saxatilis♀
Syn. *Alyssum saxatile*
Gold dust
Compact evergreen sub-shrub forming a low hummock of grey-green foliage. In late spring bears dense clusters of small, bright yellow flowers.
height & spread: 20x20cm
A. saxatilis 'Citrina'♀ Pale lemon-yellow flowers.

A. saxatilis 'Flore Pleno' Double flowers.
cultivation: Site in full sun. Water moderately and feed monthly. Clip back after flowering to keep in shape.

Crocus chrysanthus
'Elegance'
Cormous perennial flowers in early spring. Has bright golden-yellow flowers with brown feathering on the outer petals.
height: 7.5cm
C. chrysanthus 'Gipsy Girl' Pale yellow with clear purple feathering.
C. 'Dutch Yellow'♀ Large-flowered cultivar.
cultivation: Plant in autumn in John Innes No.1 with extra grit. Place corms at a depth of 7.5cm, in sun or shade. Keep the compost moist but avoid water-logging. Mice and voles eat young crocus corms.

Hyacinthus orientalis
Hyacinth
'City of Haarlem'♀
Bulb producing erect spikes of up to 40 bell-shaped, fragrant flowers.
height: 20cm
H. orientalis 'Yellow Hammer' Creamy yellow.
cultivation: Plant in autumn, 10cm deep in John Innes No.2, in sun or partial shade.

Narcissus
Daffodil
'Tête-à-tête'♀
Dwarf bulb producing up to 3 dainty flowers a stem.
height: 15cm
N. 'Bantam'♀ Yellow petals, orange-red central cup.
N. 'February Gold'♀ Golden flowers to 7.5cm across.

height: 30cm
N. 'Jumblie'♀ Dwarf daffodil. Deep gold trumpet with pale yellow reflexed petals.
cultivation: Plant bulbs in autumn at a depth of one-and-a-half times their own height in free-draining compost. Site in sun or dappled shade.

Water moderately. No need to feed. After flowering the bulbs may be planted in open ground. Prone to fungal infections in wet compost. Narcissus fly may damage bulbs.

Rhododendron
'Princess Anne'♀
Compact and rounded dwarf evergreen shrub bearing clusters of funnel-shaped, pale yellow flowers. Pale green leaves are bronze when young.
height & spread: 75x75cm
R. 'Patty Bee'♀ Very free-flowering. The leaves turn bronze in winter.
cultivation: Plant in autumn in ericaceous compost and add slow-release fertiliser. Site in sun or light shade. Water liberally, especially in dry weather, preferably with rainwater. Trim as necessary after flowering to maintain a compact shape. Mulch in autumn with leaf-mould.

Summer

Abutilon
Flowering maple
'Canary Bird'♀
Twiggy shrub with bell-shaped flowers and glossy, evergreen leaves.
height & spread:
1.2mx60cm

cultivation: Grow in John Innes No.3 with organic matter added. Water freely and feed while growing. Lightly prune to shape in spring and pinch out tips to promote bushiness. Over-winter in a warm greenhouse.

Allium moly
Golden garlic
'Jeannine'♀
Bulb producing up to 40 starry flowers in exuberant large loose clusters.
height: 30cm
A. flavum♀ Pendant clusters of small flowers with prominent stamens.
cultivation: Plant bulbs in autumn at a depth of twice their height. Use John Innes No.2 with added organic matter. Water while growing, avoiding excessive winter wet. Apply a balanced liquid feed once the buds form.

Argyranthemum
Marguerite
'Jamaica Primrose'♀
Vigorous evergreen sub-shrub with finely dissected, grey-green leaves, and pale yellow daisy-like flowers with darker yellow eye.
height & spread: 75x75cm
A. 'Cornish Gold'♀ Has mid-green foliage.
cultivation: Site in full sun. Water freely in summer but keep almost dry in winter. Feed fortnightly. Cut off dead flower stalks.

Asarina procumbens
Creeping snapdragon
Evergreen perennial with trailing stems and pale yellow 'snapdragon'-shaped flowers.

height & spread: 10x60cm
A. procumbens 'Nuria'
Dwarf, good for small pots.
cultivation: Site in partial
shade. Water well in spring
and summer. Keep just
moist in winter.

Asteriscus maritimus

Low-growing perennial
with rosettes of grey-green
leaves and large, bright
yellow, daisy-like flowers.
height & spread: 15x20cm
cultivation: Plant in spring
in free-draining compost
and site container in full
sun. Water moderately in
summer but protect from
excessive winter wet.
Apply a balanced liquid
fertiliser monthly in the
growing season. Deadhead
to prolong flowering. Good
for seaside gardens.

Bidens ferulifolia

Slender-stemmed
spreading perennial,
usually grown as an
annual. Bears abundant
star-shaped flowers among
finely divided, ferny foliage.
Particularly suitable for
hanging baskets.
height & spread: 30x45cm
cultivation: Plant out after
the last frosts in a good-
quality potting mix. Site
in full sun. Fairly drought-
tolerant but likes some
water. Give a liquid tomato
feed every 3 weeks. Pinch
out tips for bushiness.

Calceolaria integrifolia
Slipper flower
'Sunshine' ♀
Compact perennial sub-
shrub, usually grown as an
annual, producing a mass
of rounded yellow flowers.
height & spread: 25x25cm

C. integrifolia 'Gold Bunch'
Produces large, golden-
yellow flowers.
cultivation: Plant out after
last frosts in a good-quality
potting mix. Site in sun or
partial shade. Keep the
compost moist at all times,
and apply a liquid tomato
feed every 3 weeks.

Celosia argentea
'Century Yellow'
Upright annual bearing
striking conical, feathery
plumes of bright golden-
yellow flowers.
height & spread: 50x20cm
C. argentea 'Kimono Yellow'
Dwarf variety, 20cm tall.
cultivation: Plant out after
the last frosts into a moist
but free-draining compost.
Needs sheltered site in sun.

Coreopsis verticillata
'Zagreb'
Bushy perennial with
finely divided, fern-like
leaves and abundant,
starry blooms.
height & spread: 40x30cm
C. grandiflora 'Domino'
Upright plant. Daisy-like
flowers with ragged petals.
height & spread: 25x20cm
cultivation: Plant out in late
spring in full sun. Water
moderately. Deadhead to
prolong flowering.

Gazania
'Kiss Yellow'
Compact, bushy perennial
with abundant daisy-like
flowers with a brown
circle around the eye.
height & spread: 25x25cm
G. 'Daybreak Yellow' Bright
yellow flowers with dark
central eyes.
G. 'Talent Yellow' ♀ This plant
has silvery grey foliage and

pure yellow flowers.
cultivation: Plant out in
early summer in free-
draining compost. Site in
full sun as flowers close in
dull weather. Gazanias are
drought-tolerant but do
better if watered. Protect
from winter cold.

Helianthus annuus
Sunflower
'Moonwalker'
Fast-growing, upright
and branching annual,
has several large flowers
with light yellow petals
and dark brown centres.
height & spread:
1.2mx50cm
H. annuus 'Pacino' Dwarf
annual bearing several
small-centred, bright
yellow flowers.
height & spread: 60x20cm
H. annuus 'Sunbeam'
Dwarf, has golden-yellow
flowers with greenish
centre.
cultivation: Grow in free-
draining fertile compost in
full sun. Water generously
and feed every 3 weeks.
The dwarf varieties do not
need staking.

Helichrysum italicum ♀
Curry plant
Hardy evergreen sub-
shrub with narrow, silvery
grey, aromatic leaves.
Tight, flattened clusters of
mustard-yellow flowers.
height & spread: 60x60cm
H. 'Schwefellicht'
Herbaceous perennial with
grey, woolly foliage and
clusters of fluffy flowers.
cultivation: Plant in spring
in John Innes No.2 with
extra grit and site in full
sun. Water moderately

throughout summer,
keeping compost just moist
in winter. Remove flower-
heads once they have
faded, and prune any frost-
damaged shoots in spring.

Hemerocallis
Day lily
'Eenie Weenie'
Compact and free-
flowering perennial with
arching, linear leaves and
exotic lily-like flowers, each
lasting just one day, held
on upright stems.
height & spread: 25x40cm
H. 'Little Gypsy Vagabond'
Evergreen; pale yellow
flowers with purple eyes.
H. 'Yellow Lollipop' Very
narrow leaves and large
bright yellow flowers.
cultivation: Plant in spring
in pots of John Innes No.3
with added organic matter
such as leaf-mould. Site in
full sun. Water freely while
growing and apply a
balanced liquid feed every
2 weeks from spring until
the buds form. Divide
clumps every 2 years in
spring to maintain vigour.
Slugs may attack young
foliage in spring.

Lilium
Lily
'Connecticut King'
Strong-growing bulb
producing as many as
15 upward-facing,
star-like flowers.
height: 90cm
L. 'Grand Cru' Upward-
facing flowers with an
orange 'brush mark' at
base of each petal.
cultivation: Plant bulbs in
autumn at a depth of twice
their height. Use John
Innes No.2, putting a good

layer of crocks in the base of the pot. Site in a sunny sheltered position, keeping roots shaded. Water freely and give a high potash feed monthly. Store bulbs in their pots over winter, or store in boxes of damp sand in a cool place.

Lysimachia nummularia
Creeping Jenny

Vigorous, creeping evergreen perennial. Trailing stems bear saucer-shaped flowers and small, heart-shaped leaves.
height & spread: 5x45cm
L. nummularia 'Aurea'♀ Has golden-yellow foliage.
cultivation: Plant in spring and allow stems to trail. Site in sun or part shade. Keep compost moist.

Rudbeckia hirta
'Sonora'

Stout, branching perennial usually grown as an annual. Daisy-like flowers are golden-yellow with a maroon eye and a broad maroon band encircling it.
height & spread: 40x30cm
R. hirta 'Goldilocks' Semi-double with a black eye.
R. fulgida 'Goldsturm' Daisy-like golden flowers with brown centres.
height & spread: 60x30cm
cultivation: Plant in spring in a moisture-retentive compost. Site in sun and water freely, especially in hot weather. Deadhead to prolong flowering.

Santolina chamaecyparissus♀
Cotton lavender

Dense, rounded evergreen sub-shrub with tiny white

woolly leaves and pompom flowers on slender stems.
height & spread: 50x50cm
cultivation: Plant in spring in a free-draining compost. Site in full sun. Water moderately and feed once a month.

Sedum spathulifolium
'Cape Blanco'♀

Mat-forming perennial with fleshy stems and a white bloom on the central rosettes of silvery leaves. Clusters of star-shaped flowers are held just above the foliage.
height & spread: 10x20cm
S. kamtschaticum var. *ellacombeanum*♀ Compact with large pale yellow flowers.
cultivation: Plant in spring in free-draining compost in full sun. Drought-tolerant but do better with moderate watering. No need to feed. Cut off faded flower stems. Protect plants from excessive winter wet: prone to rot in wet conditions.

Tagetes patula
French marigold
'Aurora Yellow'

Fast-growing, bushy, upright annual with aromatic divided leaves and double flowers.
height & spread: 20x15cm
T. patula 'Naughty Marietta' Single, deep yellow flowers, with a maroon blotch at base of petals.
T. erecta 'Antigua Primrose' African marigold with fully double pompom flowers on erect plants.
height & spread: 20x15cm
cultivation: Plant out after

the last frosts in John Innes No.2 and site in full sun. Water moderately and apply a balanced liquid feed every 2 weeks. Deadhead to prolong period of flowering.

Zinnia
'Short Stuff Gold'

Low-growing, floriferous annual with double flowers.
height & spread: 20x20cm
cultivation: Plant out after the last frosts into well-drained compost. Site in full sun. Water moderately and apply a liquid tomato feed every 2 weeks. Deadhead to prolong flowering.

Autumn

Kniphofia
Red hot poker, torch lily
'Ice Queen'

Herbaceous perennial with numerous, tubular flowers, packed densely together at the top of sturdy flower stalks. The flowers are pale creamy yellow tinged with green, which age to creamy white.
height & spread: 1.2mx60cm
K. 'Bee's Lemon' Lemon-yellow flowers emerge from greenish buds.
height & spread: 90x60cm
K. 'Little Maid'♀ Ivory blooms are tipped with soft yellow.
height: 55cm
cultivation: Plant in autumn in a free-draining compost. Site in sun or light shade. Water moderately and feed monthly in the growing season. Remove dead flower spikes and foliage

in winter. Thrips may mottle the foliage in hot, dry summers.

Sternbergia lutea

Bulbous perennial producing rich yellow, crocus-like flowers on short sturdy stems, and long, bright green, strap-like leaves.
height: 15cm
cultivation: Plant bulbs 10cm deep in late summer, using John Innes No.2 with extra grit. Site in full sun. Water sparingly while growing – overwatering can rot the bulbs – and allow the pots to dry out completely as the bulbs become dormant. These plants need a warm summer dormancy in order to flower. Resume watering in late summer.

Winter

Eranthis hyemalis♀
Winter aconite

Tuberous perennial with yellow cup-shaped flowers tops ruff of divided leaves.
height & spread: 15x15cm
cultivation: In autumn, soak tubers overnight before planting 5cm deep in humus-rich compost. Or plant eranthis in leaf in spring. Site in sun or partial shade. Allow tubers a period of dry dormancy in summer.

Jasminum nudiflorum♀
Winter jasmine

Small bright yellow flowers carried on slender, leafless stems on this scrambling deciduous shrub.
height & spread: 1.5x1.5m

cultivation: Plant in autumn in large pots of John Innes No.3. Site in sun or partial shade. Water freely in summer and less in winter. Feed monthly in the growing season. Provide some support for the scrambling stems. Prune out about a third of the shoots in spring.

Blue-purple flowers

Spring

Anemone blanda
'Ingramii'♀

Clump-forming tuberous perennial with irregularly lobed leaves and deep blue, daisy-like, flowers.

height & spread: 15x15cm
A. blanda 'Violet Star' Violet-coloured flowers.
A. blanda 'Blue Mist' Pale blue flowers.
cultivation: In autumn, plant the tubers 5cm deep in free-draining compost. The tubers should first be soaked overnight. Site the pot in full sun. Water moderately while growing, but cease as foliage dies back. Either keep tubers dry in their pots, or lift and store them in a box of dry sand during summer. Replant and start watering in autumn. Increase by careful division of tubers.

Clematis alpina
'Pamela Jackman'

Robust and free-flowering deciduous climber bearing pendent, 4-petalled deep blue flowers with cream anthers. Flowers followed by fluffy seed heads.

height & spread: 2.4x2.4m
C. alpina 'Frances Rivis'♀ Bears mid-blue flowers with twisted petals.
cultivation: Plant in early spring in large pots of John Innes No.3 with added organic matter such as leaf-mould. Ideally, select a site where the pot, but not the plant, is in shade.

Water moderately while growing, applying a balanced liquid feed monthly in the growing season. Provide some support, such as a trellis, pergola, or another shrub, for the tendrils to cling to. Prune lightly after flowering until the plant outgrows its space or becomes straggly. Then it can be cut back hard.

Crocus tommasinianus♀
'Ruby Giant'

Early spring flowering corm has large, rounded, rich purple flowers with orange stamens.

height: 10cm
C. vernus 'Purpureus Grandiflorus' Intense violet flowers; free-flowering.
cultivation: Plant in autumn in John Innes No.2 with extra grit. Place corms very close together at a depth of 7.5cm. Site in sun or shade. Keep the compost moist but avoid waterlogging. Mice and voles eat newly planted crocus corms.

Hyacinthus orientalis
Hyacinth
'Delft Blue'♀

Bulb producing erect spikes of up to 40 bell-shaped, fragrant flowers.

height: 20cm
H. orientalis 'Blue Jacket'♀ Very dark blue flowers with purple veins.
H. orientalis 'Ostara'♀ Violet-blue flowers.
cultivation: Plant in autumn 10cm deep in John Innes No.2. Position in sun or partial shade and water moderately while growing, but avoid excessive winter wet. Hyacinth bulbs are best discarded after one season and bought fresh each autumn as the second year's flowering is usually poor. Prone to various rots and moulds.

Muscari armeniacum♀
Grape hyacinth

Bulb produces dense, erect spikes of tiny, bright blue flowers. The linear leaves appear before the flowers the preceding autumn.

height: 20cm
M. armeniacum 'Blue Spike' The tiny bell-like flowers are double.
M. azureum♀ Has pale blue flowers.
cultivation: Plant the bulbs 5-7.5cm deep in John Innes No.2 in summer. Site in sun or partial shade. Water moderately while growing. Feeding is unnecessary.

Bulbs are best planted out in the open ground once leaves start to wither, as next year's flowering in pots is usually poor.

Myosotis sylvatica
Forget-me-not
'Blue Ball'♀

Compact and rounded biennial with hairy leaves and small, saucer-shaped flowers held in dense clusters.

height & spread: 15x15cm
M. sylvatica 'Blue Basket' Taller forget-me-not with a more erect habit.
height & spread: 25x25cm
M. sylvatica 'Ultramarine'♀ Deep indigo-blue flowers.
cultivation: Plant in autumn in humus-rich compost. Site in light shade.

Water moderately. Feeding is unnecessary. Sow seed in their containers in early summer or allow to self seed. Susceptible to aphids and to powdery mildew in a dry spring.

Summer

Agapanthus campanulatus
African lily
'Isis'

Clump-forming perennial with arching, strap-like leaves. Trumpet-shaped flowers are held in loose, rounded clusters on long stalks.

height & spread: 75x45cm
A. campanulatus ssp. *patens*♀ Pale blue flowers on shorter plants.
A. caulescens♀ Mid-blue flowers on tall plants.
height & spread: 1.2mx60cm
cultivation: Grow in large pots of John Innes No.3 in full sun, sheltered from wind. Water freely from spring to autumn, but keep almost dry in winter. Apply a balanced liquid feed from spring until the flower buds form. Divide congested clumps to increase.

Ageratum houstonianum
Floss flower

'Champion Blue'

Compact annual bearing large clusters of powder-puff flowers.

height & spread: 15x15cm

A. houstonianum 'Atlantic Plus' Very dark blue flowers.

A. houstonianum 'Blue Danube' This plant is very compact and vigorous.

cultivation: Plant out after the last frosts in a good-quality potting mix and site in full sun. Water generously in the growing season and apply a liquid tomato feed every 3 weeks. Regular dead-heading will prolong flowering.

Allium schoenoprasum
Chives

Bulb producing edible, onion-scented leaves and spherical heads of papery, pale purple flowers.

height: up to 30cm

A. cyaneum♀ Pendent, violet flowers in loose, rounded clusters.

A. sikkimense Rounded clusters of blue flowers. height: 10-25cm

cultivation: Plant bulbs in autumn at a depth of twice their height. Use John Innes No.2 with added organic matter such as leaf-mould. Water moderately while growing, but avoid excessive winter wet. Apply a balanced liquid fertiliser once the buds form. After flowering, bulbs are best lifted and planted out in the open ground. Increase by dividing congested clumps.

Brachyscome iberidifolia
Swan river daisy

Bushy, spreading annual with finely dissected foliage. The abundant, fragrant daisy-like flowers are usually violet or blue with a yellow eye.

height & spread: 30x45cm

B. iberidifolia 'Blue Star' The unusual petals are curled to form 'quills'.

B. iberidifolia 'Brachy Blue' Dwarf variety, blue flowers.

height & spread: 15x15cm

cultivation: Plant out after the last frosts in a good-quality potting mix. Site the container in sun or partial shade. Water moderately and apply a liquid tomato feed every 3 weeks. Deadhead to prolong flowering.

Campanula isophylla♀
Italian bellflower

Trailing perennial which is usually grown as an annual. It bears masses of pale mauve-blue, star-shaped flowers on short stalks, and has heart-shaped leaves borne on trailing stems.

height & spread: 20x30cm

C. isophylla 'Stella Blue' Violet-blue flowers.

cultivation: Plant out after the last frosts in a good-quality potting mix. It should be sited in full sun or in partial shade.

Water freely while the plant is growing, applying a balanced liquid feed monthly. Deadheading regularly will help to prolong the length of the flowering period.

Felicia amelloides
Blue Marguerite

'Santa Anita'♀

Bushy evergreen sub-shrub which is usually grown as an annual. The daisy-like, yellow-eyed, light blue flowers are carried on slender stalks above the bright green, oval leaves.

height & spread: 30x40cm

F. amelloides 'Santa Anita Variegated'♀ Has cream-splashed leaves.

cultivation: Plant out after the last frosts in a good-quality potting mix and site the containers in full sun. These marguerites should be watered generously and given a balanced liquid feed every 2 weeks. Pinch out young plants to encourage bushiness. Cut off dead flower stalks to prolong flowering.

Heliotropium arborescens
Heliotrope, cherry pie

'Marine'♀

Compact evergreen sub-shrub with dark green leaves and bearing dense clusters of richly fragrant purple flowers.

height & spread: 45x45cm

H. arborescens 'Chatsworth'♀ Vigorous with very fragrant flowers.

H. arborescens 'Dwarf Marine' Compact has height and spread of just 30cm.

cultivation: Plant out after the last frosts in a good-quality potting mix. Site in full sun. Water moderately, applying a balanced liquid feed monthly. Remove faded flowerheads. May be overwintered in a frost-free greenhouse.

Hydrangea macrophylla

'General Vicomtesse de Vibraye'♀

This deciduous shrub has large, glossy, serrated leaves and dense, rounded, mop head flowers of clear mid blue, provided that they are grown in acid compost.

height & spread: 1.2x1m

H. macrophylla 'Mariesii Perfecta'♀ Syn. 'Blue Wave' Has rich blue 'lacecap' flowerheads in acid compost.

cultivation: Plant in autumn in large pots of ericaceous compost. The flowers will be pink if a neutral or limey compost is used.

Site in partial shade with some shelter from cold, drying winds. Water generously while growing, using rainwater if possible (because tap water is alkaline), and feed every month. You could also add a blueing compound to guarantee blue flowers. Top-dress annually in autumn with garden compost or leaf-mould. In the spring, prune back the stems to just a strong pair of buds.

Ipomoea tricolour
Morning glory

'Heavenly Blue'

Fast-growing, twining annual with heart-shaped leaves and funnel-shaped flowers with a white throat.

height & spread: 2.4x1m

I. purpurea Has mauve to purple flowers.

cultivation: Plant out after the last frosts in a good-quality potting mix and site in full sun. Provide support for the climbing stems, such as a wigwam of canes or a trellis against a wall. Water freely and apply a balanced liquid feed monthly.

Lavandula angustifolia
Lavender
'Hidcote' ♀

Compact, bushy shrub with aromatic, grey-green leaves and small, purple flowers held in short, dense spikes.

height & spread: 60x60cm
L. stoechas ssp. *pedunculata* ♀ (French lavender) Fragrant flowers topped with conspicuous purple-pink bracts.

cultivation: Plant in spring in John Innes No.2 and site in full sun. Once established, lavender is reasonably drought-tolerant but for best results plants should be watered moderately.

Apply a balanced liquid feed monthly. Clip off faded flower spikes in autumn. Prune lightly in spring to maintain bushiness.

Lobelia erinus
'Riviera Blue Splash'
Compact, bushy annual forming low mounds. The fan-shaped flowers are a pale lilac-blue.

height & spread: 10x10cm
L. erinus 'Blue Fountains' Vigorous trailing type with a profusion of pale blue flowers.
L. erinus 'Kathleen Mallard' Double flowered form that must be raised from cuttings.
L. erinus 'Regatta Sky Blue' It has a trailing habit and

an abundance of pale blue flowers.

cultivation: Plant out after the last frosts in a good-quality potting mix. Site the plants in sun or light shade. Keep moist at all times – the compost should never dry out.

Apply a liquid tomato feed every 2 to 3 weeks. Occasionally clip the plants over, and remove any faded flowerheads in order to encourage further flowering.

Petunia
'Purple Wave'
Vigorous, bushy and spreading Multiflora type with abundant, weather-resistant, magenta flowers.

height & spread: 40x50cm
P. 'Daddy Blue' Grandiflora type with large, silver-blue flowers, variegated with dark blue veins.
P. 'Frenzy Blue' This Multiflora type petunia bears purple flowers.

cultivation: Plant out into containers after the risk of frost has passed, selecting a sheltered site in full sun.

Use a good-quality potting mix. Water plants freely and apply a liquid tomato feed every 2 weeks.

Deadhead all petunias regularly. Large-flowered (Grandiflora) types should have some shelter as their flowers may get damaged by wind and rain.

Salvia splendens
'Salsa Purple'
Bushy annual with dense spikes of long, tubular flowers emerging from very conspicuous dark purple bracts.

height & spread: 25x20cm
S. farinacea 'Rhea' (Mealy sage) Tall, slender spikes of dark purple flowers. Densely branched stems are covered by a white 'mealy' dust.

height & spread: 35x20cm
cultivation: Plant out after the last frosts in a good-quality, moist but free-draining compost. Site in full sun to light shade. Water liberally while growing and apply a liquid tomato feed fortnightly. Remove faded flowerheads regularly.

Scaevola aemula
Fan flower
'Blue Wonder'
Evergreen perennial, usually grown as an annual, with lax stems and distinctive lilac-blue fan-shaped flowers.

height & spread: 30x50cm
cultivation: Plant out after the last frosts in a good-quality potting mix and site in sun or partial shade.

Water plants moderately while growing and apply a liquid tomato feed every 2 to 3 weeks. Pinch out the tips of young plants to encourage bushiness.

Solenopsis axillaris
Syn. *Isotoma axillaris,*
Laurentia axillaris
'Blue Stars'
Woody sub-shrub, almost spherical in habit, bearing a profusion of starry, pale violet-blue flowers.

height & spread: 30x30cm
cultivation: Plant out in a free-draining compost after the last frosts. Site in full sun. Water moderately and feed monthly in the

growing season. Deadheading will help to prolong flowering. Overwinter in a frost-free greenhouse or conservatory.

Trachelium caeruleum ♀
'Passion in Violet'
Upright, branching perennial which is usually grown as an annual. The tiny violet flowers are borne in large domed clusters.

height & spread: 60x30cm
cultivation: Plant out after the last frosts in a good-quality potting mix and site the containers in full sun. Water the plants moderately while growing, applying a weak tomato fertiliser every 2 weeks. Deadheading will help to prolong flowering.

Verbena x hybrida
'Imagination'
This spreading and mound-forming dwarf perennial is usually grown as an annual. It bears dense, domed clusters of deep, violet-blue flowers.

height & spread: 20x30cm
V. x hybrida 'Quartz Blue' White-eyed violet flowers.
V. x hybrida 'Tapien Purple' Has a cascading habit.

cultivation: Plant out after the last frosts in full sun. Water freely, especially in dry spells and feed once a month.

Autumn

Billardiera longiflora ♀
Climbing blueberry
Evergreen, wiry-stemmed, twining climber. Shiny,

purple, oval fruits preceded by tubular yellowy green flowers in summer.
height & spread: 1.5x1.5m
cultivation: Grow in pots of ericaceous compost in a sheltered, lightly shaded position. Provide support for the twining stems by using a trellis against a wall, for example.

Water freely while the plants are growing, applying a balanced liquid fertiliser monthly. Top-dress in spring with ericaceous compost. Trim lightly in spring as needed.

Hebe
'Autumn Glory'
Evergreen shrub forms a mound of rounded leaves and bears abundant short spikes of purple flowers.
height & spread: 60x60cm
H. 'Mrs Winder'♀ Produces long spikes of violet-blue flowers. Young leaves turn dark purple in winter.
height & spread: 90x90cm
cultivation: Plant in spring or autumn in pots of John Innes No.3. Site in full sun. Water freely in the growing season and apply a balanced liquid feed monthly. Prune shrubs lightly to shape in spring if necessary. These plants are prone to powdery mildew.

Liriope muscari♀
Evergreen perennial with tufts of dark green, grass-like leaves. Small purple, bell-shaped flowers borne in dense upright spikes.
height & spread: 30x45cm
L. exiliflora Has narrower leaves and taller, lavender-blue flowers.
L. muscari 'Gold Banded'

Compact plant with leaves edged in yellow.
cultivation: Plant in spring in free-draining, humus-rich compost. Site in full or partial shade. Water liriopes moderately until established; they are drought-tolerant thereafter. Apply a balanced liquid feed monthly. Remove faded flower spikes and old leaves regularly as new foliage emerges.

Plumbago auriculata♀
Leadwort
Climbing evergreen shrub bearing rounded clusters of sky-blue flowers.
height & spread: 1.5x1.5m
cultivation: Grow in pots of John Innes No.3. Provide support, such as a trellis, for the whippy stems. Tying in will be necessary. Site containers in a lightly shaded, sheltered spot. Water the plants moderately and apply a balanced liquid feed monthly in the growing season. Shorten back flowering shoots after they have finished blooming. May be hard pruned in spring if it is outgrowing its space. Overwinter in a frost-free greenhouse.

Winter

Primula vulgaris
Primrose
'Quantum Blue'
Very early flowering evergreen perennial producing violet-blue, saucer-shaped flowers with a yellow eye.
height & spread: 20x20cm
P. vulgaris 'Danova Purple'

Large, pale purple flowers.
cultivation: Plant in early winter in humus-rich compost and site pots in a position where they will gain maximum winter sun. Water moderately and apply a balanced liquid fertiliser once buds are formed. Remove spent flowers to prolong the flowering period. Increase by dividing vigorous clumps in early spring.

Viola x wittrockiana
Winter pansy
'Universal Purple'
Low-growing perennial, usually treated as an annual. It produces large, velvety, dark purple flowers. Will continue to flower throughout winter in mild spells.
height & spread: 16x20cm
V. x *wittrockiana* 'Sorbet Blue Heaven' Violet-blue flowers.
V. x *wittrockiana* 'Ultima True Blue' Violet-blue blooms with a yellow eye.
cultivation: Plant in autumn in a good-quality, free-draining compost and site in sun or light shade. Water freely in dry spells.

Remove any dead flowerheads regularly to prolong blooming. May be eaten by slugs and snails.

Foliage

Spring & summer

Acer palmatum
Japanese maple
'Garnet'♀
Mound-forming deciduous tree with deeply and finely

cut dark purple-red palmate leaves.
height & spread: 2x2m
A. palmatum var. *dissectum*♀ The green leaves turn red, then yellow in autumn.
A. palmatum 'Red Pygmy'♀ Upright with linear leaves that are dark red in spring, green in summer and yellow in autumn.
cultivation: Plant in spring or autumn in large pots of John Innes No.3. Site in partial shade with protection from cold winds and late frosts, which may damage foliage. Water freely while growing, applying a balanced liquid feed monthly from spring to midsummer. Prune out any weak or damaged branches in winter. Prone to aphids and mites, and leaf scorch in exposed positions.

Atriplex hortensis var. rubra
Purple orache
Fast-growing, erect annual with reddish stems and purple-green foliage.
height & spread: 90x30cm
cultivation: Plant out after the last frosts in a good-quality potting mix. Site the containers in full sun in a sheltered position.

Water freely and apply a balanced liquid feed every month. Seeds can be sown directly into their container in late spring.

Chlorophytum comosum
Spider plant
'Vittatum'♀
Popular evergreen perennial with arching,

linear leaves, striped white along the centre. May produce a series of plantlets on arching stems.
height & spread: 30x30cm
C. comosum 'Variegatum' ♀
Leaves have white margins.
cultivation: Plant out in early summer. Site in sun or light shade. Water freely and feed monthly in the growing season. Overwinter indoors on a sunny windowsill.

Helichrysum petiolare
'Variegatum' ♀
Trailing perennial, usually grown as an annual, with oval, felted, silvery green leaves, each with a dark green central blotch marking.
height & spread: 30x60cm
H. petiolare 'Limelight' ♀
Yellowy green leaves.
cultivation: Plant out after the last frosts in a good-quality potting mix at the edge of a container or basket, so that the trailing stems can hang down. Site in full sun but do not allow the compost to dry out.
 Apply a balanced liquid feed every 2 or 3 weeks. Pinch out the tips of young plants to promote bushiness.

Hosta
Plantain lily
'Halcyon' ♀
Clump-forming perennial with glaucous, grey-blue, heart-shaped leaves.
height & spread: 40x50cm
H. 'Golden Prayers' Deep yellow leaves are cupped and puckered. Prefers a shady position.
H. 'Golden Tiara' ♀ Leaves

are mid green with irregular bright yellow margins.
cultivation: Plant in spring or autumn in large pots of John Innes No.2 with added organic matter. Site in light shade. Yellow-leafed cultivars generally colour best with some exposure to sun. Shelter from cold, drying winds.
 Water freely while growing, never allowing the compost to dry out, and feed in mid spring and midsummer. Mulch annually in spring with leaf-mould. Hostas are particularly prone to attack from slugs and snails.

Iresine herbstii
'Aureoreticulata'
Short-lived, erect branching perennial with succulent red stems. The oval, pointed leaves are marked with yellow along the veins.
height & spread: 40x30cm
I. herbstii 'Brilliantissima' Has rich crimson leaves with pink veins.
cultivation: Plant in early summer in pots of John Innes No.2 in full sun for best leaf colour. Water freely and apply a balanced liquid fertiliser monthly. Pinch out tips of young plants for bushiness. Overwinter indoors.

Mentha gracilis
Ginger mint
'Variegata'
Spreading perennial with reddish upright stems is clothed in ginger-scented, oval leaves that are marked with yellow.
height & spread: 30x30cm

M. suaveolens 'Variegata' (Pineapple mint) Vigorously spreading with wrinkled greyish green leaves that are irregularly marked in cream.
cultivation: Plant in spring in a moisture-retentive compost. Site in full sun, but be careful not to allow the compost to dry out. Apply a balanced liquid feed in spring and summer. All plants are easily increased by division.

Ocimum basilicum var. purpurascens
Sweet basil
Bushy aromatic annual. Its reddish purple leaves can be used in cooking.
height & spread: 30x30cm
cultivation: Plant out after the last frosts in a good-quality potting mix. Site the containers in a sunny, sheltered position. Water freely, especially in dry spells. Pinch out flower-heads as they appear to encourage more leaf production. You can sow basil seed straight into the pot in early summer. Basil is prone to slug damage.

Perilla frutescens var. crispa ♀
Vigorous annual with broadly oval, dark purple, frilly margined leaves.
height & spread: 90x30cm
cultivation: Plant out in spring in fertile, moist but free-draining compost in sun or partial shade. Water freely, applying a balanced liquid feed monthly. Pinching out the tips of young plants will encourage bushiness.

Plectranthus madagascariensis
Swedish ivy
'Variegated Mintleaf'
Creeping tender perennial with firm fleshy oval leaves, smelling of mint when crushed. The leaves are mid green with scalloped edges and white margins.
height & spread: 20x40cm
P. forsteri Oval, dark green, scallop-edged leaves; prostrate, trailing stems.
cultivation: Plant out hardened-off plants after the danger of frost has passed, using a good-quality potting mixture. Site the container in sun or light shade.
 Pinch out the growing tips of young plants to encourage bushiness. Swedish ivy may be overwintered indoors.

Ricinus communis
Castor-oil plant
'Impala'
This fast-growing, erect evergreen shrub, usually grown as a half-hardy annual or as a conservatory plant, has striking foliage. The large, palmate, reddish purple leaves are 25cm across.
height & spread: 1.2x1m
R. communis 'Zanzibarensis' The reddish purple leaves have white veins.
cultivation: Plant out after the last frosts in John Innes No.2 with added organic matter, such as leaf-mould. Site in full sun.
 Water plants freely and apply a balanced liquid feed every 3 weeks. Ricinus tends to self-seed. NB Seeds are poisonous.

Senecio cineraria

Syn. *Cineraria maritima*

'Silver Dust'♀

Evergreen sub-shrub usually grown as an annual with deeply divided, almost white, felted leaves.

height & spread: 30x30cm

S. cineraria 'Cirrus' Silvery grey lobed oval leaves.

cultivation: Plant out hardened-off plants in spring, in a good-quality potting mix. Site in full sun.

Water lightly and feed monthly with a balanced liquid feed. Snip out flower buds as they form.

Solenostemon

Syn. *Coleus* 'Royal Scot'

Flame nettle

'Royal Scot'♀

Upright bushy evergeen perennial with square stems bearing long, deep red, notched triangular leaves marked with yellow-green margins.

height & spread: 50x50cm

S. scutellarioides 'Wizard Series' Compact and bushy cultivars with foliage variously marked with shades of red, yellow, pink, purple and cream.

height & spread: 20x30cm

cultivation: Plant out hardened off plants after the last frosts into a good-quality potting mix. Site the plant in full sun (ensuring there is some shelter from the midday sun) or in a spot with light shade.

Water freely and apply a fertiliser that is high in nitrogen once a month. Pinch out growing tips to promote bushiness, and pinch out the flower buds as soon as they appear.

All year round

Aucuba japonica

Spotted laurel

'Crotonifolia'♀

Easily grown evergreen shrub with glossy leaves heavily splashed with yellow. Red berries may be produced in autumn on female plants.

height & spread: 1.2x1.2m

A. japonica f. longifolia♀ This female plant has long, narrow, pale green leaves.

cultivation: Plant in spring or autumn into John Innes No.3. Aucuba is tolerant of sun or shade. Water moderately and apply a balanced liquid fertiliser monthly in the growing season. Trim to size and shape in spring.

Buxus sempervirens

Box

'Marginata'

This slow-growing, dwarf evergreen shrub forms a low mound of small dark green leaves with strongly marked yellow margins.

height & spread: 1x1m

B. sempervirens 'Suffruticosa'♀ Dense shrub with bright green leaves, good for formal clipping.

cultivation: Plant in spring or autumn in John Innes No.3. Site in partial shade. Water freely, especially while becoming established. Feed monthly in the growing season. Trim in summer.

Chamaecyparis lawsoniana

'Aurea Densa'♀

Dwarf evergreen conifer with a rounded, conical habit. The foliage is made of tiny greeny gold scale-like leaves.

height & spread: 1.2mx90cm

C. lawsonia 'Gimbornii'♀ Forms a neat, dense blue-green globe shape.

C. lawsonia 'Pygmaea Argentea'♀ Silver-tipped, bluish foliage; likes shade.

cultivation: Plant in John Innes No.3 in full sun. Water well. Trim lightly in summer.

Chamaerops humilis♀

Dwarf fan palm

Small palm producing a crown of palmate leaves held on prickly stems.

height & spread: 90x90cm

cultivation: Grow in pots of John Innes No.3, putting plants outdoors only after the last frosts. Site in a sunny, sheltered position. Water freely and apply a balanced liquid feed monthly in the growing season. Reduce watering and move to a greenhouse over winter and cut away dying leaves.

You can produce more plants by growing suckers in small pots. Red spider mite, scale and mealy bugs may be a problem for palms grown under glass.

Cordyline australis

Cabbage tree

'Torbay Dazzler'

Erect, palm-like evergreen, with linear, arching leaves which have cream and grey-green stripes running through. It gradually develops a trunk.

height & spread: 1.8x1.8m

C. australis 'Purple Tower' Has dark purple leaves.

cultivation: Plant in spring in pots of John Innes No.3 and site in full sun. Water freely while establishing, after which it is drought-tolerant. Feed in mid spring and midsummer. Gently pull away dead leaves from the base of the trunk. In cold areas during winter, give plants the shelter of a house wall.

Erica carnea

Alpine heath

'Foxhollow'♀

Low-growing, spreading evergreen shrub with tiny, linear leaves. The foliage is yellow with bronze tips which deepens to reddish orange in very cold weather. Bears purplish pink flowers from winter to mid spring.

height & spread: 15x40cm

E. carnea 'Golden Starlet'♀ Has lime-green foliage turning a glowing yellow in summer; white flowers.

E. carnea 'Vivellii'♀ Bronze foliage; magenta flowers.

cultivation: Plant in autumn in ericaceous compost. Site pots in full sun. Water freely and apply a weak liquid fertiliser once a month in growing season.

Clip the flower spikes back once they have gone over. Grey mould (botrytis) may develop in warm, wet conditions.

Euonymus fortunei

'Silver Queen'♀

Upright, evergreen shrub has glossy oval leaves, with broad creamy white margins that are tinted rose in winter.

height & spread: 90x90cm

E. fortunei 'Emerald 'n' Gold'♀ Spreading habit;

with bright green, yellow-edged leaves.

E. fortunei 'Emerald Cushion' Compact and mound forming plant with lustrous dark foliage.

height & spread: 30x30cm
cultivation: Plant in John Innes No.2. Site in sun for best leaf variegation. Shelter from cold winds. Water moderately and feed monthly in the growing season. Lightly prune in late spring. Cut out shoots of variegated plants that have reverted to green.

Fatsia japonicaa
Syn. *Aralia japonica*

Slow-growing, rounded evergreen shrub with large, glossy, dark green palmate leaves. In autumn it bears round clusters of creamy white flowers.

height & spread: 1.5x1.5m
F. japonica 'Variegata' ♀
The leaves are margined with cream at the tips of the lobes.

cultivation: Plant in spring in large pots of John Innes No.3. Site in sun or partial shade and shelter from cold, drying winds.

Keep the compost moist throughout summer, but drier in winter. Apply a balanced liquid feed in spring and summer. Fatsia does not need pruning, but can be trimmed to shape in spring.

Glechoma hederacea
Ground ivy
'Variegata'
Vigorous evergreen perennial with trailing stems. The leaves are kidney-shaped, with scalloped margins,

irregularly marked with white blotches. Especially suited to hanging baskets.

height & spread: 15x90cm
cultivation: Plant in spring in a good-quality potting mix. Site in sun or partial shade. Position plants so that stems can trail down. Water freely while growing and give a balanced liquid feed monthly.

Hedera helix
Ivy
'Glacier'
Easily grown and adaptable evergreen that can be encouraged to either climb or hang down. The five-lobed leaves are mottled green and silvery green and have narrow white margins.

height & spread: 1x1m *H. helix* 'Cavendishii' ♀ Large, 3-lobed leaves, mottled with grey. The leaf margins are cream.
H. helix 'Golden Easter' Light green leaves with an irregular yellow margin.

cultivation: Plant in spring or autumn in pots of John Innes No.3. Site containers or baskets in sun or light shade: although ivies tolerate deep shade, their leaf variegation will be less pronounced if deprived of sun. Water freely in dry spells. Apply a balanced liquid feed monthly in the growing season. Clip plants to shape, in spring.

Juniperus horizontalis
Juniper
'Emerald Spreader'
Slow-growing dwarf conifer, low and spreading in habit. Small, needle-like leaves are bright green.

height & spread: 30x80cm
J. communis 'Compressa' ♀ Dwarf, slow-growing variety, conical in habit with grey-green foliage.
height & spread: 80x45cm
J. squamata 'Blue Star' ♀ Compact rounded bush with silvery blue foliage.
height & spread: 40x80cm
cultivation: Plant in autumn in John Innes No.3. Choose a site in full sun. Water well while establishing; after this, junipers are fairly drought-tolerant. Pruning is rarely necessary unless the plant is outgrowing its space.

Laurus nobilisa
Bay laurel, bay tree, sweet bay
Striking evergreen shrub or tree with dark green, glossy, aromatic foliage used in cooking. Bay tolerates clipping and is commonly shaped into formal round-headed (lollipop) or pyramid-shaped standards.

height & spread:
1.2mx80cm
L. nobilis 'Aurea' ♀ Golden-yellow foliage best in late winter and early spring.
cultivation: Plant in spring or autumn in John Innes No.3. Site in full sun to partial shade. Shelter from cold, drying winds. Clip to size or shape in summer. Prone to scale insect, leaf spot and sooty mould.

Nandina domestica ♀
Sacred bamboo
Evergreen or semi-evergreen shrub forming a clump of erect, leafy stems, looking similar to bamboo. The leaves are reddish

purple when young, becoming green in summer and turning red in winter. In midsummer, sprays of creamy white, starry flowers appear. After a hot summer, the flowers are often followed by a vigorous show of bright red berries.

height & spread: 90x75cm
cultivation: Plant in spring in John Innes No.3. Site in full sun in a sheltered spot. Water moderately and apply a balanced liquid feed in spring and summer. Prune out old or weak shoots in spring.

Ophiopogon planiscapus
Lily turf, mondo grass
'Nigrescens' ♀
Clump-forming, evergreen grass with dark, purplish black leaves, dark purple flowers and black fruits.

height & spread: 25x30cm
O. jaburan 'Vittatus' Taller growing plant with green leaves margined and striped cream.

height & spread: 60x30cm
cultivation: Plant in spring in John Innes No.2 with added organic matter, such as leaf-mould. Site pots in sun or partial shade. Water moderately while growing, but sparingly in winter. Apply a balanced liquid feed in spring and summer. Mulch with leaf-mould in autumn.

Phormium
New Zealand flax
'Sundowner' ♀
Clump-forming evergreen perennial making a tuft of rigid, upright, pointed linear leaves. These are

green-bronze in colour with pink margins.

height & spread: 1.2x1m

P. 'Dazzler' Arching bronze leaves with red, orange and pink stripes.

P. tenax 'Variegatum' ♀ Dark green leaves with yellow stripes and margins.

cultivation: Plant in John Innes No.3 in a sunny, sheltered spot. Water freely in summer but sparingly in winter. Apply a liquid feed in spring and summer.

Pittosporum tenuifolium
'Purpureum'

Evergreen shrub or small tree with lustrous, wavy-edged, dark purple leaves.

height & spread: 1.5x1m *P. tenuifolium* 'Abbotsbury Gold' Green leaves with dark margins and yellow midribs.

P. tenuifolium 'Silver Queen' ♀ Grey-green leaves with white margins.

cultivation: Plant in spring in John Innes No.3. Site in full sun for best leaf colour. Shelter from cold, drying winds. Water well while establishing; after this, plants are drought-tolerant. Keep almost dry in winter. Apply a balanced liquid feed in spring and summer. Scale insects may be troublesome.

Pleioblastus auricomusa
Syn. *Arundinaria auricoma* Bamboo

A bamboo producing upright, branching, purplish canes clothed in lance-shaped leaves. The leaves are bright yellow with dark and pale green stripes running through.

height & spread: 1.2mx60cm

P. gramineus Arching canes bearing abundant grass-like, drooping, mid-green leaves.

P. pygmaeus Dwarf bamboo with bright green leaves held horizontally.

height & spread: 20x30cm

cultivation: Plant in spring or autumn in large pots of John Innes No.3 with added leaf-mould. Shelter from strong winds and site variegated varieties in full sun; other varieties prefer light shade. Water liberally, especially while establishing. Apply a balanced liquid feed monthly in the growing season. Canes that have flowered will die off, so prune these out.

Sempervivum
Houseleek
'Rubin'

Clump-forming, evergreen perennial, with rosettes of fleshy foliage. These leaves are flushed bronze-red. At flowering, the rosette elongates into a fat leafy spike bearing many starry pink flowers.

height & spread: 7.5x7.5cm

S. arachnoideuma (cobweb houseleek) Leaf tips are crisscrossed with fine, cobweb-like hairs.

S. tectoruma Green leaf rosettes flushed red.

cultivation: Plant in spring in a light, free-draining compost in full sun.

Though sempervivums are drought-tolerant, water moderately. No need to feed. *S. arachnoideum* should be protected from excessive winter wet. Easily increased by planting offsets.

Thymus
Thyme
'Doone Valley'

This mat-forming evergreen sub-shrub has small aromatic dark green leaves splashed with yellow. Purple-pink flowers are borne in dense heads in summer.

height & spread: 13x35cm

T. serphyllum 'Annie Hall' (Creeping thyme, wild thyme) Mat-forming aromatic plant with shell-pink flowers.

T. vulgaris 'Silver Posie' Upright and shrubby plant bearing white margined green leaves.

height & spread: 20x20cm

cultivation: Plant in spring in a free-draining compost and site in full sun. Water moderately while growing. No need to feed. Clip over after it has flowered to keep a compact shape.

Yucca filamentosa
'Bright Edge' ♀

Stemless evergreen shrub forming a rosette of stiffly erect, linear, dark green leaves with broad yellow margins. Bears tall plumes of creamy white flowers.

height & spread: 60x75cm

Y. whipplei Dense tufts of slender grey-green leaves.

cultivation: Plant in spring in John Innes No.2. Site in a sunny position sheltered from the wind. Although yuccas are drought-tolerant, they should be watered moderately in summer and sparingly in winter. Feeding is not necessary. After flowering the leaf rosettes die off, although varieties of *Y. filamentosa* produce offsets. Protect from severe frosts in colder areas.

Page references in *italic* indicate illustrations.

A

abelia 103
abutilon 27, 108, 114
acer 120
acid-loving (ericaceous) plants 40-1, 85
aconite *78*, 79, 116
African daisy 109
African marigold 103
agapanthus 27, 100-1, 117
agave *86*
ageratum 118
ajuga 83, 101
alchemilla mollis *51*, *69*, *69*
all-year-round planting schemes 66-7
alpines 48-9, 84
alyssum 42, 102, 106, 114
amaryllis 76-7, *77*
anemone 42, 50, 55, 100, 117
animal pests 97, *97*
antirrhinum 104, 108-9
aphids 96, *96*
aromatic plants 46
asarina *14*, 114-15
aster 107, 110
asteriscus *49*, 115
atriplex 120
auricula 74
autumn planting schemes 70-3
azalea 40, *41*

B

bamboo *45*, 50, 123, 124
basil *30*, 31, 121
bay 24, 31, 46, 123
begonia *14*, 16, 17, 95
berberis *25*, 42
bidens 17, 47, 115
black-eyed Susan 17, 113

blueberries 32, *33*, 119-20
bougainvillea *47*
box *15*, 42, 45, 122
brachyscome 16, 118
brugmansia 101
bulbs 54-5, 78-9, 97
busy lizzie 15, 16, 17, 26, 50, 68-9, *69*, 112

C

cabbages, ornamental *35*, 42, 67, 72
cachepots 11
camellia 82, 104, 108
campanula *16*, 17, 42, 118
candytuft 48, 102
canna lily 110-11, 113
Cape marigold 101
castor-oil plant 121
celosia 115
ceramic and glazed containers 13
Chilean glory vine 46, 112
chilli peppers 109
chives 31, 118
Christmas planting schemes 76-7
chrysanthemum 70, *70*
clematis 11, 42, *43*, 117
climbing plants 24, 46, 50
colour schemes 18-21, 24, 26
compost 85, 88, 98
  acid-loving plants 40, 85
  alpines 48
  bulbs 78
  fruit 32
  lime-loving plants 42
  moisture-loving plants 44
  soil-free composts 85
concrete containers 12
conifers *14*, 24, 122
containers
  drainage 10, 44, 84, *84*, 85, 88
  insulation 95

materials and textures 12-13
  planting 88-91
  securing 24
  sizes and shapes 10-11, 82
  stability 10
convolvulus 101
cordyline 27, 122
coreopsis 115
cosmos 47
cotoneaster *25*, 42
courgettes *35*
creeping Jenny 11, 116
creeping zinnia 113
crinum 103, 107
crocus 42, 50, *66*, 67, 78, *78*, 100, 114, 117
cucumbers 34
cup flower 102
cup and saucer vine 101
cuphea 111-12
curry plant 115
cyclamen 15, *25*, 50, 70, 107, 111

D

daffodil 19, 20, 50, 54, *54*, 55, 78, *78*, 114
dahlia 11, *47*, 109, 112
daisies 19, 42, 70, 104, 107-8
day lily 112, 115
dead nettle 100
deadheading 95
dianthus (pink) *20*, 42, 43, 48, 63, 63, 105
diascia 15, *47*, 105, 112
drainage 10, 44, 84, *84*, *85*, 88
drought-loving plants 46-7

E

epimedium 111
euonymus 122-3

F

fan palm 122
fatsia 50, 123
felicia 16, 101, 118
ferns 15, 26, *45*, 50, *51*
fertilisers 42, 48, 66, 94, 98-9
flame nettle 122
flower balls 90-1
forget-me-not 117
foxglove 51
French marigold *47*, 113, 116
front door, pots at the 24-5
fruit 26, 32-3, 72-3
fuchsia 15, 17, 24, 25, 27, 50, 95, 105
fungicides/insecticides 94-5, 99

G

gaillardia 109
galvanised metal containers 13, 22
gardenia 62
gaultheria 40, 73, 107
gazanias 19, 112, 115
geranium (cranesbill) 24, 50
geranium (pelargonium) *14*, 16, 17, 27, *27*, 46, 64-5, *64*, 109-10
gerbera 20, 61
ginger lily 101-2
glass-fibre containers 12, 13
golden garlic 114
grasses 11, 45, 46, *57*, 74
gunnera 44, 45, *45*

H

hanging baskets 16-17, 23, 24, 64
 flower balls 90-1
 planting 90-1

heathers *14*, 20, 40, 71, *72*, 73, 103, 107, 122
hebe 42, *43*, 120
helichrysum *16*, 17, 46, 47, 121
heliotrope 118
hellebore 50, *56*, *57*
herbs 26, 30-1, 84
heuchera 17, *17*, 50, 70, 71
hosta 50, *51*, *61*, 121
hyacinth 54, *54*, 58, 114, 117
hydrangea *41*, 50, 105, 118
hygiene 98

I J K

informal displays 22-3
iresine 121
iris 19, 42, *45*, 67, 79
ivies 11, 15, 17, 26, 50, *56*, *57*, 67, 121, 123
jasmine 26, 116-17
juniper 42, 123
kniphofia 116

L

laurel 50, 122
lavatera 105
lavender 19, *20*, *47*, 66, *66*, 119
lettuces 36, *37*
lilies 11, *25*, 50, 63, *63*, 69, *69*, 102, 106, 112-13, 115-16
lime-loving plants 42-3
liriope *56*, 120
lobelia *14*, 15, 17, *27*, 50, 64, *69*, 106, 119
love-lies-bleeding 108

M

Madagascar periwinkle 105

magnolia 40, 100
marguerite 24, 47, 70, 101, 104, 114, 116
marigold 19, 36, 44, *47*, 103, 111, 113
mask flower 108
Mediterranean plants 42, 46, 84
mimulus (monkey flower) 50, 109, 113
mint 121
moisture-loving plants 44-5
morning glory 46, 47, 118-19
mulches 46, 48, 86-7, 96
muscari 117
myrtle 102

N

nasturtium 16, 17, 19, *20*, 36, 37, *37*, 46, 47, 110
nemesia *61*, 113
nemophila 48, 102
nerine 107
nigella 48

O

ophiopogon *74*, 123
orchid 76-7
osteospermum *47*, 102
over-wintering plants 95

P

painted/decorated containers 22
pansy 74-5, *74*, 114, 120
parrot's beak 109
patios 26-7
penstemon 27, 106
peppers, ornamental 72, *72*, 73
perilla 121
perovskia *43*, 84

pests and diseases 94-5,
96-9
petunia 15, 16, *16*, 17,
27, *51*, 60-1, *61*, 63,
63, 95, 119
philadelphus 26
phormium 123-4
pieris 40, 100
pittosporum 124
plant selection 82-3
planting containers
88-91
plastic containers 12,
28
plumbago 70, 120
poached egg flower 48
poinsettia 76
polyanthus *15*, *54*, 56-7,
56, *57*
poppy *20*, 42, 47
primula *14*, 50, 56, *56*,
57, *57*, 104, 120
pyracantha 113

R

ranunculus 44, 50, 104,
108, 111
rhododendron 40, 85,
114
rhubarb 32, *33*
rose 62-3, *63*, *66*, 67,
95, *99*, 106, 110
rudbeckia 42, *47*, 116

S

sage 26, 31, 42, *43*
salads 36-7
salvia 110, 119
santolina 116
sarcococca 103
scaevola 17, 119
sedum 46, 48, 116
sempervivum (houseleek)
46, 48, *49*, 124
senecio 47, *56*, 67, 122

shade-loving plants 50-1
skimmia 40, 111
slipper flower 115
slugs and snails 96, *96*
snowdrop 79, 103
solenopsis 119
solenostemon 122
spider plant 120-1
spring planting schemes
54-9
spruce *76*, 77
sternbergia 116
stock 42, 62
stone and reconstituted
stone containers 12,
22, 28
strawberries 32, *33*
succulents 46, 48, 49,
49, 84
summer planting schemes
60-5, 68-9
sunflower 112, 115
sutera *69*, 102-3
sweet william 71

T

terracotta containers
12, 22, 24, 28
thrift 104-5
thyme 26, *30*, 31, 46,
63, 124
tobacco plant (nicotiana)
26, 47, 50, 62, 63,
106, 109
tomatoes 26, 34, *35*, 109
trachelium 119
trailing plants 17
tropaeolum tuberosum
113-14
tulip 20, 42, 58-9, *58*, 78,
78, 100, 104, 108, 111

V

vegetables 26, 34-5, 72-3
verbena 16, 17, 64, 106,

110, 119
Versailles planters 11, 24
viburnum 42, 46, 103-4
vine weevils 97, *97*
viola 17, 17, 36, 42, 66,
66, 67, 74, *74*

W

wallflower 42, *43*, 70,
108, 111
water features 28-9
water-retaining gels
90, 92, *93*
watering 92-3, 99
acid-loving plants 40
hanging baskets 16
lime-loving plants 42
self-watering pots 92
window boxes 14
window boxes 14-15
winter jasmine 116-17
winter planting schemes
74-9
winter protection 95
wisteria 46
wood and wicker
containers 12, 13,
22, 28

Y Z

yucca 42, 46, *61*, 124
zinnia 47, 106-7, 113,
116

Acknowledgments

The position of photographs and illustrations on each page is indicated by letters after the page number: **t** top; **b** bottom; **l** left; **r** right; **c** centre

Cover © Reader's Digest/Linda Burgess **1** © Reader's Digest/Debbie Patterson **2-3** © Reader's Digest/Debbie Patterson **4 l** © Reader's Digest/Debbie Patterson **r** © Reader's Digest/Debbie Patterson **5 l** © Reader's Digest/Debbie Patterson **r** © Reader's Digest/Jason Smalley **6** © Reader's Digest/Debbie Patterson **8-9** © Reader's Digest/Debbie Patterson **10** © Reader's Digest/Debbie Patterson **11 t** © Reader's Digest/Debbie Patterson **bl** © Reader's Digest/Debbie Patterson **br** © Reader's Digest/Debbie Patterson **12 tr** © Reader's Digest **cl** www.primrose-london.co.uk **bl** © Reader's Digest/Debbie Patterson **br** www.primrose-london.co.uk **13 tl** © Reader's Digest **br** © Reader's Digest/Debbie Patterson **tr** www.primrose-london.co.uk **cl** www.primrose-london.co.uk **14 tr** © Reader's Digest/Debbie Patterson **cr** John Glover **bl** John Glover **br** © Reader's Digest/Debbie Patterson **15** © Reader's Digest/Debbie Patterson **16 l** © Reader's Digest/Debbie Patterson **r** © Reader's Digest **17** © Reader's Digest **18** © Reader's Digest **19** © Reader's Digest/Debbie Patterson **20 l** © Reader's Digest/Linda Burgess **r** © Reader's Digest/Debbie Patterson **21** © Reader's Digest/Debbie Patterson **22** © Reader's Digest **23** © Reader's Digest **24 t** © Reader's Digest/Debbie Patterson **b** © Reader's Digest/Debbie Patterson **25 l** © Reader's Digest **r** © Reader's Digest **26** © Reader's Digest **27** © Reader's Digest **28** © Reader's Digest, © Reader's Digest **29** © Reader's Digest/Debbie Patterson **30 l** iStockphoto.com/Emiliane Maria Maniaci **31** iStockphoto.com/Hazel Proudlove **32** The Garden Collection/Liz Eddison The Garden Collection/Liz Eddison **33 r** © Reader's Digest/Debbie Patterson **34 bl** Gap Photos Ltd/J S Sira **34-35** Gap Photos Ltd/Friedrich Strauss **35 r** © Reader's Digest/Debbie Patterson **36** © Reader's Digest/Debbie Patterson **37 tr** © Reader's Digest/Debbie Patterson **br** The Garden Collection/Liz Eddison **tl** Gap Photos Ltd/Amanda Darcy/West Dean Gardens **38-39** © Reader's Digest/Debbie Patterson **41 l** The Garden Collection/Gary Rogers **r** © Reader's Digest/Debbie Patterson **42** © Reader's Digest/Joanna Walker **43 t** © Reader's Digest/Debbie Patterson **bl** © Reader's Digest/Debbie Patterson **br** © Reader's Digest/Nick Clark **44** © Reader's Digest/Debbie Patterson **45** © Reader's Digest/Debbie Patterson **46 t** © Reader's Digest/Debbie Patterson **b** © Reader's Digest/Debbie Patterson **47** © Reader's Digest/Debbie Patterson **49 tl** © Reader's Digest/Debbie Patterson **tr** © Reader's Digest/Debbie Patterson **b** The Garden Collection/Marie O'Hara **51 t** © Reader's Digest/Debbie Patterson **bl** © Reader's Digest/Debbie Patterson **br** © Reader's Digest/Jason Smalley **52-53** © Reader's Digest/Debbie Patterson **54** © Reader's Digest/Debbie Patterson **55** © Reader's Digest/Debbie Patterson **56 l** © Reader's Digest/Debbie Patterson **c** © Reader's Digest/Linda Burgess

r © Reader's Digest/Debbie Patterson **57** © Reader's Digest/Debbie Patterson **58** © Reader's Digest **59** © Reader's Digest **60** © Reader's Digest **61 l** © Reader's Digest **r** © Reader's Digest **62** © Reader's Digest **63** © Reader's Digest **64 l** © Reader's Digest/Debbie Patterson **r** The Interior Archive/Simon McBride **65** © Reader's Digest/Debbie Patterson, © Reader's Digest/Debbie Patterson **66** © Reader's Digest/Linda Burgess **67** © Reader's Digest/Linda Burgess **68 l** © Reader's Digest/Debbie Patterson **bc** Jerry Harpur/Lisette Pleasance **68-69** © Reader's Digest/Debbie Patterson **69** © Reader's Digest/Debbie Patterson **70 l** © Reader's Digest/Debbie Patterson **r** © Reader's Digest/Debbie Patterson **71** © Reader's Digest/Debbie Patterson **72** © Reader's Digest/Debbie Patterson **73** © Reader's Digest/Debbie Patterson **74 l** © Reader's Digest/Debbie Patterson **r** © Reader's Digest/Debbie Patterson **75 l** © Reader's Digest/Debbie Patterson **r** © Reader's Digest/Debbie Patterson **76 l** © Reader's Digest/Debbie Patterson **r** © Reader's Digest/Debbie Patterson **77** © Reader's Digest/Debbie Patterson **78 l** © Reader's Digest/Debbie Patterson **r** © Reader's Digest/Debbie Patterson **79 t** © Reader's Digest/Debbie Patterson **b** © Reader's Digest/Debbie Patterson **80-81** © Reader's Digest/Jason Smalley **82 l** © Reader's Digest **r** © Reader's Digest **83 tr** © Reader's Digest/Debbie Patterson **cr** © Reader's Digest/Debbie Patterson **bc** © Reader's Digest/Debbie Patterson **br** © Reader's Digest/Debbie Patterson **c** © Reader's Digest **84 bl** © Reader's Digest/Debbie Patterson **br** © Reader's Digest/Debbie Patterson, © Reader's Digest/Debbie Patterson **tl** © Reader's Digest/Debbie Patterson **tc** © Reader's Digest/Debbie Patterson **85 bl** © Reader's Digest/Debbie Patterson **br** © Reader's Digest/Debbie Patterson **tl** © Reader's Digest/Debbie Patterson **cl** © Reader's Digest/Debbie Patterson **86** © Reader's Digest/All Debbie Patterson except for broken plate by Joanna Walker **87** © Reader's Digest/All Debbie Patterson except for handful of shells by Alex McDonald **88 l** © Reader's Digest/Debbie Patterson **r** © Reader's Digest/Debbie Patterson **89 tl** © Reader's Digest/Debbie Patterson **tr** © Reader's Digest/Debbie Patterson **br** © Reader's Digest/Debbie Patterson **bl** © Reader's Digest/Debbie Patterson **90 bl** © Reader's Digest/Debbie Patterson **br** © Reader's Digest **l** © Reader's Digest/Debbie Patterson **91 t** © Reader's Digest **bl** © Reader's Digest **br** © Reader's Digest/Debbie Patterson **92 l** © Reader's Digest **r** © Reader's Digest **93** © Reader's Digest **94 l** © Reader's Digest **c** © Reader's Digest **r** © Reader's Digest **95 l** © Reader's Digest **r** © Reader's Digest **96 t** iStockphoto.com/John Keay **b** iStockphoto.com/Joseph Hoyle **97 t** iStockphoto.com/AtWaG **c** iStockphoto.com/Frank Kirkegaard **b** iStockphoto.com/John L Richbourg **98** Gap Photos ltd/Friedrich Strauss **99 t** Garden World Images **tc** Frank Lane Picture Agency/Nigel Cattlin **bc** Garden Picture Library/Christi Carter **b** Photos Horticultural Picture Library

---

Reader's Digest Container Gardening is based on material in *Reader's Digest Container Gardening for All Seasons* published by The Reader's Digest Association Limited, London

First Edition Copyright © 2007

The Reader's Digest Association Limited, 11 Westferry Circus, Canary Wharf, London E14 4HE **www.readersdigest.co.uk**

Editor Lisa Thomas
Art Editor Kate Harris
Proofreader Barry Gage
Indexer Marie Lorimer

Reader's Digest General Books
Editorial Director Julian Browne
Art Director Nick Clark
Managing Editor Alastair Holmes
Head of Book Development Sarah Bloxham
Picture Resource Manager Sarah Stewart-Richardson
Pre-press Account Manager Sandra Fuller
Senior Production Controller Deborah Trott
Product Production Manager Claudette Bramble

Origination Colour Systems Limited, London
Printed and bound in China by CT Printing

We are committed to both the quality of our products and the service we provide to our customers. We value your comments, so please feel free to contact us on **08705 113366**, or via our website at **www.readersdigest.co.uk**

If you have any comments about the content of our books, email us at **gbeditorial@readersdigest.co.uk**

ISBN 978 0 276 44206 3
BOOK CODE 400-614 UP0000-1
ORACLE CODE 250010674H.00.24